Nick Vandome

Digital Photography For Seniors

For the Over 50s

In easy steps is an imprint of Computer Step
Southfield Road · Southam
Warwickshire CV47 0FB · United Kingdom
www.ineasysteps.com

Notice of Liability
Every effort has been made to ensure that this book
contains accurate and current information. However,
Computer Step and the author shall not be liable for
any loss or damage suffered by readers as a result of
any information contained herein.

Trademarks
All trademarks are acknowledged as belonging to their
respective companies.

Printed and bound in the United Kingdom

ISBN-13 978-1-84078-321-6
ISBN-10 1-84078-321-4

Contents

1 Joining the digital club

Everything is going digital and cameras are no exception. This chapter offers an introduction to digital photography.

Why this book?

The expansion of digital photography has been remarkable: from being an expensive curiosity only a few years ago, it has now become the primary way in which people capture photographs. With this has come a similar growth in the number of books about digital photography. These cover a wide range of topics and most of them are aimed at all groups of users.

However, few books on digital photography concentrate specifically on the needs and requirements of seniors, who are perhaps new to the subject and all of its associated jargon and technology.

The aim of this book is to cut through some of the more complex areas of digital photography and focus on making the process of taking and using digital pictures as straightforward and satisfying as possible. With this in mind the book will cover many specific tasks connected with digital photography. These will include:

- Choosing the right digital camera, including issues such as the size of the camera and also the size of the camera's screen

- Taking better pictures, concentrating on popular areas such as holiday photographs and family shots

Don't forget

Age is no barrier to digital photography and the technology is not as daunting as it may at first seem.

- The best and quickest ways to transfer digital photographs from a camera to a computer

- Simple editing techniques for quickly improving the appearance of digital photographs:

Don't forget

For further details of working with photo editing programs, see Chapter Eight.

- Sending and receiving digital photographs by email

- Sharing digital photographs on the Internet so that they can be viewed from locations worldwide:

Don't forget

For further details of using photos with email and on the Internet, see Chapters Nine and Ten.

Don't forget

For further details of printing and displaying photos, see Chapters Eleven and Twelve.

- Printing and displaying photos so that you can make the most out of them once they have been taken

Comparing digital and film

Although it sometimes seems that digital photography has its own complex and jargon-laden language, the good news is that the basic process of picture-taking is remarkably similar to that of taking pictures with a film camera.

Similarities
The similarities between taking pictures with digital and film cameras include:

- With both types of media the picture can be composed through the camera's viewfinder

- In most cases, the camera focuses the photo using autofocus. This is usually done by half-depressing the shutter release button until the photo is focused

- The photo is taken by fully depressing the camera's shutter release button

- The photo is captured by light passing through the camera's lens

Differences
Despite the similarities, there are also some differences when taking pictures with a digital camera:

- In addition to a traditional viewfinder, most digital cameras also have a screen on the back of the camera that can be used for composing pictures:

Hot tip

Look for a camera that has both a screen and a viewfinder, in case it is too sunny to see the screen properly.

● Once a photo is taken on a digital camera it is stored on a memory card within the camera, rather than on film. Memory cards come in a variety of sizes and can store a certain number of images, depending on their size. Once the memory card is full, the images can be downloaded onto a computer. After this, the images can be erased and the card used again. Think of a memory card as film that can be used over and over again

● Digital photos can be viewed as soon as they have been taken, using the camera's screen. If you want to, you can also delete photos from the memory card while it is in the camera. This can be done to get rid of unwanted images and free up space on the memory card

● Digital photos provide a lot more flexibility for use once they have been taken. They can be downloaded and edited on a computer, printed, emailed to family and friends around the world or shared on the World Wide Web

Digital jargon explained

As with any form of new technology, digital photography has more than its fair share of jargon and acronyms:

- Card reader. This is a device that can be used to download photos from a memory card onto a computer. The card reader is connected to the computer via a cable. The memory card is then inserted into the card reader for downloading

- Docking station. This is another device for downloading photos. The camera is placed in the docking station and the downloading process commences automatically with the software provided. An excellent option for downloading photos with a minimum of fuss

- Downloading. The process of transferring photos from the camera to a computer or other device

- Effective Pixel Count. The actual number of pixels captured in a photo at the camera's highest setting

- File size. This is the size of a digital photo in terms of how much space it takes up on a memory card or a computer. Since digital photos are essentially just digital data they are measured in standard digital units, i.e. kilobytes or, more usually, megabytes. (Megabytes do not equate to megapixels)

- Image size. This is the physical size of the photo in terms of pixel dimensions, e.g. 3220 pixels x 2880 pixels. This size can be manipulated in a photo editing program

- JPEG. This is the most common file format for digital photos. JPEG stands for Joint Photographic Experts Group and is usually identified by a .jpg extension at the end of a filename once the photo has been downloaded

- Image sensor. This is the device inside a digital camera that captures the light once it passes through the camera's lens. It then processes the data and passes it on to the camera's memory card. In some ways an image

Beware

Digital photos from different cameras can have different file sizes, even if they have the same number of pixels. This is because cameras can compress the pixels so that the final file sizes can vary considerably.

Don't forget

Image sensors come in two formats: CCD or CMOS. The majority of cameras use the CCD version.

sensor is more like traditional film than the memory card is, even though it is not visible

- Megapixel. This is the term for a million pixels: e.g. 3 million pixels equals 3 megapixels

- Memory card. This is the card onto which photos are saved once the data has been captured by the image sensor. Memory cards are removable from the camera

- Photo editing. This is the process whereby digital photos are manipulated on a computer once they have been downloaded. There are numerous programs that can perform this task

- Pixels. The building blocks of digital photos. A pixel is a colored square that contains the digital data that helps make up the photo. The name is a contraction of Picture Element

- Resampling. This is the process whereby digital photos are made larger or smaller within photo editing software

- Resolution. A term used in a number of areas of digital photography. One definition refers to the size of a digital photo, e.g. a resolution of 6 megapixels. Another use for resolution refers to the way a photo can be manipulated to allow it to be displayed at different sizes. (For more information on this see Chapter Seven)

- Uploading. This is the process of copying photos held on your computer to another location. It is most commonly used in relation to online sharing and printing websites. If you want to use one of these services, you first have to upload your photos onto the site

- Zoom (digital). This is a function of digital cameras whereby a subject is made bigger in the viewfinder or on the screen by increasing the size of the pixels

- Zoom (optical). This is a more genuine zoom function as it makes the subject larger through the use of mirrors in the camera's lens

Don't forget

Since digital photos are just a collection of colored digital dots, it is possible to make them larger or smaller by adding or removing pixels from the photo.

Getting enough pixels

A common battle between digital camera manufacturers is what is known as the "pixel race". This is the continuing attempt to fit more and more pixels into each digital image.

Pixel is a contraction of Picture Element and pixels are the small colored squares that make up a digital photo. In general, the number of pixels in a digital image is counted in millions, or megapixels, e.g. 5 million pixels or 5 megapixels. When digital cameras are quoted as having a certain number of pixels or megapixels, this refers to the maximum number of pixels that the camera can capture in a single image. (However, this headline figure can sometimes be slightly misleading since some of the pixels are required for processing functions within the camera. The figure to look for to see the actual number of pixels in each image is known as the Effective Pixel Count and can be found in the manufacturer's specifications for the camera.)

The total number of pixels in a digital photo is calculated by multiplying the numbers for the width and height of the photo. So a photo that was 3000 pixels by 2000 pixels would have 6 million in total, or 6 megapixels.

In the early days of consumer digital cameras, 2 million pixels was considered a good value for a photo. Now, the bare minimum is 3 million pixels, with figures of 5, 6, 7 million and above becoming commonplace.

So why does it matter how many pixels are in a photo? The first thing to remember is that pixels can be captured at different qualities, so more does not necessarily equate to a better photo. Most digital cameras compress the photos to a certain degree, which involves discarding some of the unwanted digital data in each pixel. This helps to reduce the file size of each photo, even though it may still have a large number of pixels. As a rule, the more expensive the digital camera, the greater the quality of the pixels in each photo.

All things being equal though, the more pixels in a photo, the better the quality at which it can be printed. This is

Don't forget

Pixels in a digital photo are first captured on an image sensor within the camera before they are transferred to the camera's memory card. The quality of the image sensor can have more impact on the final quality of the image than the overall number of pixels.

because if there are more pixels then they can be packed more densely together and so blend into an overall image rather than appearing as individual colored blocks. If the pixels are visible it is known as a pixelated photo, which means that there are not enough pixels for it to be printed at a good quality at the selected print size.

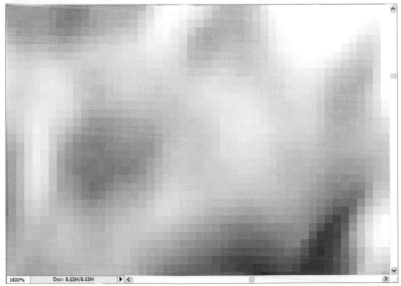

Don't forget

The two examples on this page show how a photo can be magnified in a photo editing program to display individual pixels within the photo.

Don't forget

For a detailed look at the controls on a digital camera, see Chapter Two, pages 28 and 29.

Hot tip

Viewing photos directly from the camera on a TV screen is a great way to have family slide shows, without first having to download photos onto a computer.

Around the camera

Much of the technical wizardry of a digital camera is hidden within the camera body. However, there are some important items that can be accessed externally:

Memory cards

These are inserted into a slot on the camera body. For more information about inserting memory cards, see Chapter Three.

Batteries

These are inserted in a similar way to memory cards. For more information about inserting batteries, see Chapter Three.

Camera to computer connection

Almost all digital cameras have a socket for a cable to be plugged in so that they can be connected to a computer. This can be used to download photos from the camera to the computer.

Camera to TV connection

A lot of digital cameras also have a connection for viewing photos directly on a television. The camera is connected to the television via a cable and then the photos on the camera can be viewed as a slide show:

Expanding your horizons

Once you have taken a digital photo you can use it in the same way as one from a film camera: i.e. have it printed out. This can be done at home by downloading the photo onto a computer and printing it from there, or by taking the camera's memory card into a photographic retailer and asking them to print it directly from the card. Digital photos can be printed in the traditional fashion but also onto novelty items such as T-shirts, cakes and mugs.

Sharing by email

Digital photos can quickly and easily be attached to email and instantly sent to family and friends around the world.

If you are sending digital photos by email, keep the file size relatively small so that they can be downloaded quickly. See Chapter Seven for details about making photos smaller.

Sharing on the Web

There are numerous sites on the Web where online photo albums can be created for sharing with family and friends:

...cont'd

Getting creative

Digital photos can also be incorporated into items such as cards and calendars, either by you, using a photo editing program, or through a photo retailer.

Beware

Online services charge a fee for creating items such as calendars and cards. However, you can do them yourself on a computer using a photo editing program (as with the samples on this page). For more details on this, see Chapter Twelve.

March   *2007*

Sun	Mon	Tue	Wed	Thu	Fri	Sat
				1	2	3
4	5	6	7	8	9	10
11	12	13	14	15	16	17
18	19	20	21	22	23	24
25	26	27	28	29	30	31

Happy Spring

2 Choosing a camera

This chapter looks at all the issues about getting the right camera for your needs, in terms of size, feel, screen and overall functionality.

The right camera size

One aspect of all digital devices, from mobile phones to digital cameras, is that manufacturers are continually trying to make them smaller and smaller. For some groups of users this is a desirable design feature as they do not mind having a lot of small, fiddly buttons with which to operate devices. However, for senior users, something a bit more substantial is a definite advantage as it is easier to hold steady and the controls are more accessible.

When you are looking for a digital camera it is important to find one that is not too small. There are a number of disadvantages to smaller cameras:

- It can be hard to keep the camera steady when taking photos as there is not enough of it to hold on to

- The controls can be difficult to access and operate

- The lens and flash can be more easily obscured when taking photos

Hot tip

Take some photos with any cameras that you try, so that you can get a feel for them in a proper photo-taking situation.

In general, look for a digital camera that is fairly solid and has a comfortable feel to it when you are holding it. For this reason, it is important to physically try a camera before you buy it. Sometimes cameras look suitable but they just don't feel right in your hands. From the front, the camera should look as if it will be easy to hold comfortably:

From the back, the controls should be well placed, with enough room between them:

Don't forget

The controls on a digital camera are usually situated on the top and back of the camera body.

Camera grip

Larger digital cameras tend to have a much more solid camera grip. This is the side of the camera held by the right hand and it can be an excellent way to keep the camera steady. Look for a camera grip that has a rubber surface, as this provides extra stability.

Beware

Smaller cameras, with no grip, can be harder to hold comfortably and operate efficiently. They are also more likely to get lost.

Looking for a large screen

When digital cameras first came onto the market, one of their most revolutionary features was the screen at the back of the camera. This is known as the LCD (Liquid Crystal Display) screen and it serves a dual purpose: it can be used to frame and compose photos instead of the viewfinder and it can also be used to view, or delete, photos once they have been taken.

LCD screens continue to be a vital element of digital cameras and one welcome development in recent years has been that their size has increased significantly. When looking at a digital camera, always try and find one that has a large screen (a minimum of 2 inches across). This will make it easier both for composing photos and for viewing them once they have been taken.

Beware

A few cheaper digital cameras do not have a screen, but these should be avoided.

Hot tip

Test a camera's screen in direct sunlight to see how clear, or otherwise, it is.

Using a viewfinder

Although a large screen is a definite advantage, there is one situation where it can be a distinct disadvantage. This is when the screen is so large that it takes up the whole of the back of the camera and there is no space for a traditional viewfinder. This is fine, unless you are trying to take photos in very bright or sunny conditions, in which case the glare from the sun may make it very hard to see what is on the screen. Because of this it is important to have a traditional viewfinder too, in case the screen cannot be used properly.

Look for a screen and viewfinder together:

Hot tip

Look for a viewfinder that has a rubber edge surrounding it. This will make it more comfortable and easier to look through.

23

Switching between screen and viewfinder

If a camera has a screen and a viewfinder it is only possible to use one of them at a time. To switch between the two there will be a button on the back of the camera that can be pressed to toggle between screen and viewfinder as required.

Benefits of docking stations

An important part of digital photography is getting the photos from the camera onto a computer so that they can then be edited, emailed and shared online. There are three main ways of doing this:

- Connecting the camera directly to the computer

- Removing the camera's memory card and putting it into a card reader that is connected to the computer

- Using a docking station

All of these methods are looked at in detail in Chapter Six, but serious consideration should be given to using a docking station, as this is the quickest method and involves the least effort with connecting cables or removing and inserting memory cards.

A docking station is a device that connects the camera to the computer. The docking station only has to be connected to the computer once, and then the camera can be placed in the docking station whenever you want to download photos:

Don't forget

A range of Kodak cameras come with docking stations and also dedicated printers that can act as a docking station.

Advantages

There are a number of advantages to using a docking station:

- Ease of use. Photos can be downloaded by placing the camera on the docking station and pressing a single button

- Software provided. Docking stations come supplied with compatible software. When the camera is placed on the docking station, the software recognizes it and launches automatically

25

- Recharging. In addition to downloading photos, docking stations also charge the camera's batteries, so you do not have to worry about a separate charger for rechargeable batteries

Not all digital camera makers provide docking stations for their cameras. Kodak are the main manufacturer of cameras with compatible docking stations and they also provide their own Easyshare software to use with these devices. This provides the means to download photos using the docking station and it also provides an environment for editing and organizing the photos once they have been downloaded.

Up close with zoom

Most compact digital cameras now have some form of zoom capability. This is a fairly essential feature as it enables you to make the subject of a photo appear larger without having to get closer to it. This can be useful in a number of situations:

- Portraits. Zoom can be used to fill the frame with the subject, without you having to get too close and crowd them. This will make the subject feel more relaxed

- Candid shots. These benefit from the use of zoom as it enables you to take photos of people when they are engaged in activities without them being aware of the presence of the camera. It is particularly effective with children

- Buildings. Details of buildings and architecture can be picked out through the use of zoom

- Animals. Frequently, photos of animals are disappointing as the subjects appear too small. A large zoom facility can help to solve this problem

Types of zoom

When looking at digital cameras you will be quoted two different figures, one for optical zoom and one for digital zoom. Of the two, optical zoom is much more important as it physically moves the lens's mirrors within the camera to make the subject appear larger. Digital zoom just enlarges the photo on the screen or in the viewfinder. In general, ignore the digital zoom figure and concentrate on the size of the optical zoom.

Accessing zoom

On most cameras, there is a button for accessing the zoom function. Press W (-) to give a wide-angle shot and T (+) for a telephoto shot (one where the subject appears closer).

Hot tip

Some digital cameras have a function called image stabilization. This helps to make photos as steady and clear as possible. It is particularly effective for photos taken with a high level of zoom.

Wide angle

Use wide angle when you want to get as much of a scene in the photo as possible:

Telephoto

Use telephoto when you want to get close to a subject and make it look as large as possible:

Hot tip

It is always worth taking two photos of the same scene, one with the least amount of zoom and one with greatest amount of zoom. This can produce dramatically different results.

Around the controls

Although different digital cameras will have their controls in slightly different places, most of them have very similar sets of controls to give the camera its functionality:

On-off
The on-off button is used to power the camera on and off. It usually has two options: one for accessing the photo-taking functions of the camera and one for the viewing and reviewing of photos.

Shutter release button
This is almost always situated on the top of the camera and is used to focus a photo and then capture it.

Zoom controls
As shown on the previous two pages, these are used to zoom in to, or out from, subjects in a photo.

Flash
There is usually a button to activate the flash and also a button to scroll through the options for flash, such as red-eye reduction or turning the flash off completely.

Landscape or close-up
This button can be used to specify whether you are taking a distant shot or a close-up one. If these options are selected, the camera will make the appropriate settings automatically.

Self-timer
This is usually used if you want to include yourself in a photo and need a few seconds to move into the shot.

Delete

This can be used to delete photos immediately after they have been taken. It can also be used to delete photos when they are being viewed using the camera's review function.

Menu

This can be used to access the relevant menus for the current function. For instance, if you are in photo-taking mode, the menus will apply to taking photos, and if you are in review mode they will give review options.

Review

This is used to view photos that have already been taken. It can be accessed at any time.

Camera controls

These are controls that determine the functionality of the camera. Some of the most common are:

- Auto, when the camera selects all of the settings

- Scene, when preset selections can be made for different photographic situations

- Aperture priority or shutter speed priority. This can be used by more experienced photographers if they want to set the aperture or shutter speed of the camera

- Video, which allows for short videos to be taken

Don't forget

Once a photo has been taken it is displayed briefly on the camera's screen. During this time, which is usually only a few seconds, it can be deleted using the Delete button.

Don't forget

Aperture priority mode is usually denoted by an A on the camera controls and shutter speed priority is denoted by an S.

Setting up the camera

Sometimes photography is a nice leisurely pastime: a landmark or landscape is well positioned in front of you and you have plenty of time to take the photo. However, more often than not there will be a certain degree of time constraint when taking a photo: a grandchild may be playing a game or activity that needs to be captured quickly; a sunset could be vanishing in a matter of moments; or you may want to get a photo of a fast-moving vehicle or animal. With all of these examples it is important to have the camera ready for use as quickly as possible. This means that if there are any settings that you want to specify, these should already be done before you are ready to take photos. If not, you may end up fiddling with the settings and then miss the vital picture. In most cases, it is perfectly acceptable to leave the camera on Auto, in which case it will take care of all of the picture-taking settings. However, there may be times when you want to change some of the settings manually. If you are doing this, think about the types of photos that you are going to be taking and then make the relevant settings before you start the photo-taking process. Some settings that you might want to consider changing are:

- Picture size. This is the size, in pixels, at which the photo will be captured. This will normally be shown as a megapixel size, e.g. 6 megapixels. There will be a number of different settings for this on your camera, which can be accessed from the camera's menu system. As a general rule, use the largest picture size for photos that you want to use for printing and a smaller one for photos that you are going to email or use on the Web

- Color. This will enable you to determine the color of the photo. The options range from natural and bright colors, to sepia and black & white

- Autofocus. This determines how the autofocus works. The options are usually single, in which case the autofocus only works when the shutter release button is half depressed, or continuous, in which case the camera tries to autofocus continuously

Hot tip

For more advanced functions, such as aperture and shutter speed priority, there are more settings that you can change manually.

Using the camera's scenes

A common feature on a lot of digital cameras is a choice of scene modes. These are modes that have assigned settings for specific photographic situations. So, if you are taking photos at night and are unsure of the settings to use, you could use the Night scene to simplify the process greatly.

If a camera has scene modes it will probably have quite a few of them. Some of the most common are:

- Children mode. For capturing action photos of children in bright light

- Sport mode. For capturing fast-moving action, such as sporting events

- Portrait mode. For capturing portraits against a softened background

- Landscape mode. For capturing landscapes in vivid colors. In landscape mode the focus is set to infinity

- Fireworks mode. This uses a slow shutter speed to capture the effect of fireworks at night. A tripod is essential for this type of shot as it will result in a blurred photo otherwise

...cont'd

- Backlight mode. This can be used where the main subject is in front of a brightly lit area. In this mode, the flash will fire automatically to illuminate the main subject and so equalize its lighting with the brighter background

- Close-up mode. For capturing photos at very short distances. Usually used for small objects

- Snow mode. This can be used when capturing photos in very bright conditions. In this mode, the lighting of the brightly lit areas will be exposed accurately without altering the exposure of any other objects in the photo

- Night modes. There are usually a couple of night modes, one for landscapes and one for portraits when you want to capture both the main subject and the background. For both of these a tripod is essential to keep the camera steady

- Museum mode. For capturing photos when you do not want the camera to make any noise, and you do not want the flash to fire. It can be used in locations such as museums or art galleries or at indoor events such as school plays

Don't forget

Always use a tripod if you are going to be taking photos at night or indoors without the use of flash.

3 Getting up and running

This chapter deals with what happens when you first start using a digital camera. It covers some of the accessories you need and shows how to take and view your first photos, and delete any you don't want.

Inserting a memory card

Memory cards are vital elements in the digital photography process. These are removable cards that are inserted into a digital camera and used to store photos once they are captured. Memory cards come in a variety of types but the good news is that you do not have to worry about the type of card that comes with your camera, as photos can be downloaded or printed from any type of memory card. When using a digital camera it is important to know how to insert, and remove, the memory card:

1. To insert a memory card, open its compartment cover on the camera

2. Push in the memory card until it clicks into place. Do not force it in

3. To remove the memory card, press the button next to the card, or press the memory card itself until it pops out

Inserting batteries

Digital cameras use a lot of battery power so it is best to choose a camera that uses some form of rechargeable batteries. Some cameras use traditional batteries that can be recharged with a battery charger, and others take solid lithium battery packs. Either type of rechargeable battery must be charged and inserted into the camera. To do this:

1. Insert the battery, or batteries, into the charger and wait until they are fully charged

2. Open the battery compartment cover on the camera (in some cases this may be the same compartment that holds the memory card)

3. Insert the battery, or batteries, according to the diagram on the battery compartment

4. Close the battery compartment cover firmly

Hot tip

If possible, use a camera with rechargeable lithium batteries.

Hot tip

Always carry a spare, fully charged, battery with you whenever you are taking photos.

35

Turning the camera on

Once the memory card and charged batteries have been inserted it is time to turn the camera on. This activates the camera's digital circuitry and prepares it for use. To do this:

Beware

Most consumer digital cameras take a few seconds to be ready for use once they have been turned on. This can be an issue if you want to take a photo very quickly.

Beware

Some cameras have an auto sleep feature where the camera will go into standby mode if it is not used for a few minutes. In some cases the camera will actually turn itself off completely.

 Before use, the camera lens will be retracted

 Press the Power button on, or move it to the on position (It is usually located on the top or back of the camera)

The camera will make some whirring and clicking sounds as it prepares itself for use

The lens will be opened and, in some cases, extended

The screen at the back of the camera will be activated and display the view through the lens

Keeping the camera steady

One problem in all forms of photography is an effect called camera shake. This is where a small amount of hand movement when a photo is being taken causes the camera to shake slightly, resulting in a fuzzy and out of focus photo. There are a number of ways to try and keep the camera as steady as possible and avoid camera shake:

1. Use a full length tripod. This is the best option for keeping the camera steady, but it can be cumbersome to carry around all the time

Hot tip

When looking at a tripod, make sure it has a good sturdy head that can hold the camera firmly in position at all times.

Don't forget

Mini-tripods are usually about six inches in height and have pliable legs that can be bent into place.

2. Use a mini-tripod. These can be bought at camera shops and are an excellent compromise between size and steadiness. They fit easily into a pocket

3. A small bean bag. This can be used instead of a tripod to steady the camera

...cont'd

4 A shoulder bag. Small bags can also be used in a similar way to a bean bag, depending what you are carrying in your bag

5 Benches or barriers. These can be used to give extra stability when taking photos:

Beware

Although benches and doorframes can give additional stability, they will not be enough to avoid camera shake in low-level lighting, such as at night.

6 Doorframes. This is another option for achieving greater stability when you are hand-holding the camera while you are taking a photo:

Taking your first shot

With the camera turned on, and steady, you are ready to take your first shot. To do this:

1. Position the camera so that you can see clearly through the screen to compose the photo

2. Compose the scene and half-depress the shutter release button to focus the shot, using the camera's autofocus. A light should appear on the screen when the shot is in focus

3. Keep the shutter release button half depressed once focus has been achieved

4. Fully depress the shutter release button to take the photo

5. The photo will be visible on the screen

Hot tip

Before you start taking photos, read the camera's manual as this will provide useful technical and picture-taking information.

Don't forget

Since you are not using up any film you can experiment extensively when you first get a digital camera and take as many shots as you like.

Getting the timing right

One ongoing issue when taking photos with a digital camera is a problem known as time lag. There are three types of time lag and they all affect the timing when taking digital photos.

Start-up time lag

This is the time that it takes a digital camera to be ready for use when it is turned on. Due to the amount of digital processing that goes on within the camera, the start-up time can be a few seconds. Obviously this can have an impact on capturing certain types of photos if your camera is not ready.

Shot time lag

This is the amount of time that it takes for a photo to be captured once the shutter release button has been pressed. This is usually only fractions of a second but it can have a significant impact on photos of moving objects or people, especially children, particularly if they move or blink just as the photo is being taken, resulting in an unflattering pose:

Recycling time lag

This is the amount of time it takes the camera to get ready for the next shot. When a photo is taken the camera has to process the information and copy it to the memory card. Depending on the efficiency of the camera this can take a few seconds. While this is happening the camera will lock and not allow you to take another photo.

Reducing time lag

Although time lag cannot be removed completely, there are a number of ways to minimize its effects:

1. Keeping your camera turned on all the time. Most cameras have a Sleep mode that will save battery power but still allow the camera to be turned on. Although there is still a slight time lag when Sleep mode is deactivated, this is not as long as the time lag for turning the camera on

2. Take several consecutive shots of a subject. This is particularly important for photos of subjects such as grandchildren as they are likely to make sudden movements. This can be done with the camera's Burst function, if it has one, where several photos can be taken consecutively while the shutter release button is still depressed:

Beware

Burst functions can use up a lot more battery power than capturing photos individually.

3. Use a good quality memory card. Memory cards copy digital data at different speeds and the faster the information is copied the quicker it is ready for the next shot. In general, the more expensive the memory card the quicker it will be

Looking at photos

As soon as photos have been taken it is possible to view them on the camera. This is an invaluable way to see how the photo has turned out and if any adjustments are required. To review photos:

1 Press the Review button on the camera

2 Photos can be viewed on the camera's screen

3 Use the zoom function on the camera to get a close-up view of parts of the photo

4 Use the buttons on the back of the camera to move through the photos that have been taken

Deleting photos

One of the great advantages of digital photography is that you can delete any photos that you do not like, directly from the camera. This can be done when a photo has just been taken or while they are being reviewed. To do this:

Don't forget

The procedure for deleting photos can vary in detail from camera to camera, but the general approach is always the same.

1 Immediately after a photo has been taken it will be displayed briefly on the camera's screen. If you do not want to keep it press the Delete button, or

delete

2 Select the Review function on the camera and select a photo you want to delete

3 Press the Delete button

4 In the Delete Confirmation window, select Picture to delete the photo

Beware

Most delete functions have an option for deleting all photos stored in the camera or on the memory card. If you select this option, make sure the photos have already been downloaded or that you definitely do not want them.

Keeping your camera safe

Although digital cameras are relatively robust externally, they have a number of delicate elements within them so it is best to try and keep them as safe as possible. To do this:

1 Buy a case for the camera to keep it safe when not in use. Make sure this fits the camera securely

2 Always use the neck strap when using the camera:

3 Keep the camera away from water. Water is one of the biggest threats to digital cameras so always try and keep them out of the rain and away from areas of water such as the sea or swimming pools. If your camera does get wet, try and dry it out completely before you use it again

4 If you are on holiday with your digital camera, keep it out of sight as much as possible, particularly in poorer countries where it may be considered an item of considerable worth

Hot tip

When you buy a digital camera the neck strap will probably not be attached. Make sure you attach the strap before you start using the camera.

4 Family and friends

Photos of family and friends are always popular. This chapter shows how to get the most out of this subject and how to improve your photos of people.

Using screen and viewfinder

Taking photos of family and friends is one of the most common, and most satisfying, uses for a digital camera. One of the great advantages is that everyone can see the photos immediately afterwards and several photos can be taken at one time, if required.

When capturing photos of family and friends there may be occasions when you want to switch between using the camera's screen and its viewfinder:

Hot tip

If you are taking group photos using the screen, it is possible to take several shots without the group being aware and posing rigidly. This can lead to more relaxed end results.

1 Use the camera's screen when capturing groups of people. This will enable you to look at them directly and talk to them in a more natural fashion while you are still composing the photo with the screen:

2 Use the viewfinder if it is important to keep the camera as steady as possible, such as for individual portraits. This is because if you use the screen the camera is further away from your body and so does not have as much support

Positioning family groups

When taking photos of family groups it is sometimes hard enough to get everyone together at the same time. However, if you manage to do this it can be beneficial to take some extra time and deliberately position family members so that the group composition is more interesting. Two possible ways to do this are:

1   Arrange people in a variety of positions – some standing, sitting, lying, or in more acrobatic poses (use the younger, more flexible family members for the more difficult poses!)

Hot tip

When capturing photos of family groups you sometimes have to be a bit bossy in order to get everyone in the positions that you require.

47

2   Arrange the group around existing objects. These can be constructed or naturally occurring. Either way, it will add an extra dimension to the family group. This is a useful technique for photos of individuals as well as groups

Including yourself

In a lot of family group shots there is usually one person missing: the photographer. At times when families are together it is important to include everyone who is there. If you are taking the photo, it is still possible to include yourself in the picture. To do this:

Hot tip

If you are including yourself in a photo outdoors you can stand the camera on an object such as a rock if you do not have a tripod available.

1 Set up the camera on a tripod

2 Arrange the group as you want them. Leave a space at one side for yourself. Take a couple of test shots to make sure that there is enough space

3 Access the camera's self timer, by pressing this button:

4 Half-depress the shutter release button to focus the camera

5   Fully depress the shutter release button to activate the self timer

6   The camera will flash during the period of the self timer. This means that the photo has not yet been taken. This should give you enough time to position yourself in the shot

7   After a set period of time (usually about 20 seconds) the self timer will take the photo

8   If you do not think you will have time to get into position, compose the photo with yourself in it and get someone else to activate the camera

Don't forget

Flash used to brighten a subject in shadow is known as fill-in flash.

Hot tip

In bright sunlight, it is better to take a photo using the flash with the subject's back to the sun, rather than with them facing the sun, as looking towards the sun will cause them to squint and look a lot less natural.

Removing shadows

When taking photos of family and friends on a bright, sunny day it is easy to think that you have the perfect conditions. However, a problem can occur – people may appear shaded despite the fact that it is sunny. This happens when the sun is behind them, causing their fronts to be in shadow. This can be rectified through the use of flash:

1   If you capture a photo of someone with the sun behind them, they will appear in shadow

2   Turn on your camera's flash and take the photo again

3   The flash lightens up the front of the subjects, giving a much more balanced effect with the bright, sunny background

Family occasions

At family occasions such as weddings, parties and anniversaries there are usually a significant number of other family members who are taking photographs. At times like this it can be a good idea to try and capture candid shots to supplement the more formal photos that will be taken.

1 Use a large zoom setting to capture photos without people realizing that you are taking their picture. This can result in a much more natural pose

51

2 Capture photos of people's reactions to things, such as when chatting informally at a party:

3 Keep your camera at your side and take photos from this angle. This will capture candid shots and also add a different perspective to the photos

Photos of grandchildren

Grandchildren can be the most satisfying of photographic subjects and also one of the most frustrating. This is because children tend to keep moving constantly and they do not always want to keep still for photographs. However, there are a number of techniques that can be deployed to try and get better pictures of grandchildren:

1 Give them something to hold on to while you are taking their photo. This will help distract their attention from posing for the photo

Don't forget

Using zoom also helps to blur the background, which is a good effect in photos of children.

2 Use the zoom to get a close-up shot, without having to get too physically close to them

3 Photograph them when they are involved in some form of activity, so that they are less aware of the camera's presence

Hot tip

Even young children are very technologically aware these days and may even be able to offer advice about the workings of digital cameras.

4 Let your grandchildren take photos of each other. This may lead to surprisingly good results

Family portraits

Portraits of individual family members make great photographs for displaying on walls or mantelpieces. In some cases these can be taken by professional photographers, but this can be expensive. Alternatively, it is perfectly possible to take your own high-quality photos of other family members. To do this:

1   Give the person plenty of warning about the photo. This will enable them to prepare themselves

2   Select a suitable location, with an attractive background

3   Take a standard shot to begin with. In this example the portrait is unacceptable as there is not enough prominence for the main subject

4   To give more prominence to the main subject, they should fill the frame more and the background should be less defined

5 Move the subject further away from the background

6 Use the maximum zoom setting to zoom in on the subject. If necessary, move further back to fit in the subject once the zoom is fully extended

Hot tip

If your camera has an aperture priority mode (A) this can be used to make the background even blurrier. To do this, set the aperture to its widest setting (i.e. its lowest f-number) and this will have the effect of throwing the background even more out of focus.

7 The high degree of zoom and larger distance between the subject and the background has the effect of throwing the background out of focus, giving more attention to the subject

Eliminating red-eye

Red-eye is a common photographic problem, caused when taking photos with the flash. When the flash is used, it reflects in the retina of the subject's eye, causing the red-eye effect. There are a number of ways to try and avoid or remove red-eye:

Beware

The red-eye reduction function on a digital camera can be disconcerting due to the double flash that occurs. If you are comfortable editing photos on the computer then this can be a better option for reducing red-eye.

1 Use the camera's red-eye reduction function. Most digital cameras have this and it works by firing an additional flash, just before the photo, with the main flash, is taken. This has the effect of reducing the reflection when the photo is taken

2 Move the subject so that they are not directly in front of the camera

3 Use a photo editing program to remove red-eye from the photo on a computer. This is a simple process and one that is available in most photo editing programs. This is usually a one- or two-step operation.

It involves zooming in on the affected area and then selecting the relevant red-eye removal tool. The red-eye can then be removed by clicking on the affected area or by dragging around it with the red-eye tool

5 Better holiday photos

This chapter offers some straightforward techniques that can be used to turn basic holiday snaps into quality photos.

Improving holiday snaps

When on holiday or traveling there are usually numerous excellent photographic opportunities. However, a lot of these opportunities can be wasted through a lack of care or attention, or the thought that "it's only a holiday snap." Through spending a little more time on each photo and employing some simple techniques it is possible to turn throwaway holiday snaps into impressive photographs.

Composing accurately

One of the most simple mistakes made when composing photos is that they are not positioned accurately. This can lead to parts of the image being cut off when the photo is captured.

To solve this problem, make sure there is a reasonable border around the main subject when you view it with the camera's screen or viewfinder. If you are using zoom, reduce the level of zoom slightly so that there is enough of a border.

Don't forget

When on holiday, take as many photos as you can: you are not using up any film and you don't know when you will next be back at that location.

Being patient

When capturing holiday snaps, it can be tempting to take a lot of photos quickly, without thinking too much about them. However, it can pay great dividends to be patient and take a bit of time over each shot. This could be something as simple as waiting for someone to move out of the way of the shot or until the sun comes out from behind a cloud:

Hot tip

Checking the daily weather forecast can give you important information that can be used for your photographic activities while on holiday.

...cont'd

Two-line grid

When taking photos on holiday, the natural temptation is to position the main subject in the middle of the shot. While this creates a perfectly acceptable photo, it is possible to move the main subject to create a more interesting composition. One way to do this is by using a two-line grid. To do this, imagine two horizontal lines across the image and position the horizon at a different line in each shot:

Don't forget

Moving the camera up or down a couple of inches can have a dramatic impact on the final photos and it is always worth trying.

60

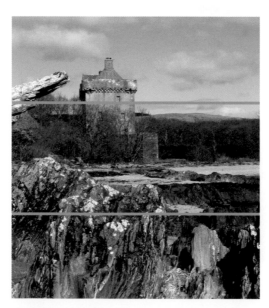

Four-line grid

Once you have mastered using a two-line grid for composing photos, you can then move on to a four-line grid. This is similar in theory but it gives more flexibility for positioning subjects within the photo, as the photo is then divided into nine sections and the main subject can be positioned in any of the sections:

Don't forget

Sometimes the best shot is with the main subject in the center of a photo, so make sure you always take some like this too.

Photographing landmarks

When on holiday some of the main photographic subjects are the local landmarks. This can be one of the most rewarding areas of photography, but some creative thought should go into the process to try and get as good a picture as possible:

Hot tip

When taking photos of landmarks, take some time to enjoy them first. Walk around them and try and see where there are good locations for taking photos, rather than snapping away as soon as you arrive.

1 Capturing a standard, straightforward photo of a landmark is perfectly acceptable

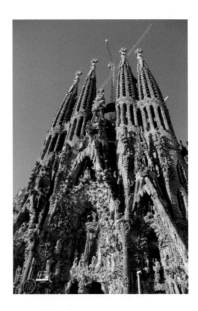

2 Include other objects in the photo to give it an extra dimension

3 Use the zoom or move in close to get some photos of the detail of a landmark

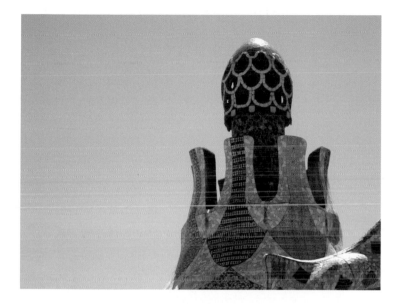

4 Capture a landmark in unusual conditions, such as stormy weather or at night

Don't forget

Most famous landmarks are illuminated at night and this can provide some excellent photographic opportunities. However, make sure you use a tripod, since the camera's flash will not be powerful enough.

Standing out from the crowd

When on holiday a good way to see a city or location is to take a tour on a bus or coach. This is ideal for sightseeing but it can be a drawback when it comes to taking photos. This is because all of the buses and coaches usually stop in the same place so you will end up taking photos in among a crowd of people and vehicles.

If you want to stand out from the crowd and take more unusual photos, a bit of effort is required. This means moving to a different location to take your photos. Move further away from the main subject so that the tourist buses and coaches are not visible. Depending on the distance, you may have to zoom in on the subject in order to fill the screen sufficiently.

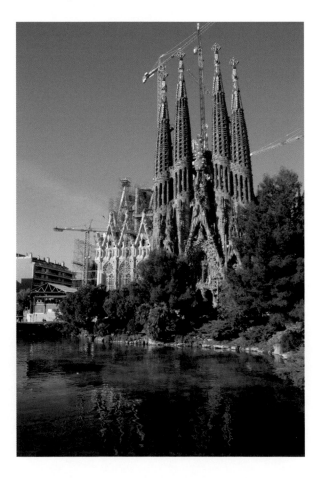

Wildlife

Photographing wildlife can be a challenge, but a very rewarding one if you get it right. The key to this type of photography is preparation, patience and getting close enough. Here are some steps to follow:

1. Before you start, make sure that your camera is working, there is enough room on the memory card and the batteries are fully charged

2. When you get to the location at which you are going to take photographs, take some time to blend in with the surroundings so that the animals become used to you. This could just involve sitting still, or stopping a vehicle on a safari

3. If your zoom is too small the wildlife will look like a speck in the distance

4. Use the maximum optical zoom available to make the animals appear as large as possible

Using sunlight

Natural sunlight is one of the best conditions under which to take photos. However, taking photos in strong sunlight, such as at midday, does not always produce the best results. This is because the light is too strong and harsh and it does not bring the maximum amount of color from a subject.

To make the best use of sunlight, photos should ideally be taken during the hour after dawn and the hour before sunset. This is when the light is not directly overhead and it creates a much richer, softer type of lighting and color. This is known as the Golden Hour and it is a time during which some excellent photos can be taken:

Beware

Never look directly into the sun with the camera's screen or viewfinder. This could damage the camera and also your own eyesight.

1 In direct sunlight a subject can appear slightly harsh with too little contrast

2 If the shot is taken during the Golden Hour, the color will be much more satisfying

3 The Golden Hour can be used to capture some very atmospheric photos

4 Sunsets can be very dramatic and this can be a good opportunity for creating silhouettes

Hot tip

To create silhouettes, keep the sunset in the middle of the photo. This will ensure the photo is exposed correctly for the sunset, thus ensuring the buildings are underexposed, i.e. very dark or black.

Night photos

Taking photos at night can produce some dramatic results and it should always be an option, particularly when on holiday. The essential thing to remember if you are taking photos of landscapes or landmarks is not to use the flash, since it will not be powerful enough to light up the scene. Instead, the camera should be put on a tripod while the photo is being taken. This is because the camera's shutter will need to be open for several seconds to allow enough light to pass into the camera. If it was being hand-held then the camera would shake and the photo would be blurred. Using a tripod can be a bit more effort but the results can be worth it:

Hot tip

When taking photos of fireworks, use a selection of shutter speeds to create different effects. To do this, select the camera's shutter speed priority mode (S) and then set the shutter speed to one second and move up in one-second steps.

6 Transferring photos

Once digital photos have been captured on a camera it is important to get them onto a computer so that they can be printed or edited. This chapter covers the ways to do this.

Using a docking station

Once you have taken photos on your camera the next step is to transfer them onto your computer. There are a number of ways of doing this, and perhaps the best option is to use a docking station as this does not involve removing the camera's memory card or connecting the camera each time you want to download images. A docking station is a device that connects to the computer; the camera is placed in the docking station to download the photos. To download photos using a docking station:

1 Place the camera in the docking station

Beware

Not all digital cameras come with docking stations: Kodak has the largest range of cameras that use them.

2 Attach the supplied cable to the docking station

Don't forget

Docking stations also charge the camera's batteries, but only after the downloading process has been completed.

3 Connect the docking station to the computer with the supplied USB cable

4 The software should recognize the docking station and the downloading process will begin

5 Once the photos have been downloaded they will be available via the software that is provided with the docking station

From camera to computer

Another option for downloading photos is to connect your camera directly to your computer. This is done with a cable that should be supplied with the camera.

Don't forget

When connecting the camera to the computer, the memory card should be left in the camera.

Beware

Connecting the camera to the computer with a cable can be a fiddly business if the USB connection is at the back of the computer.

1 Connect one end of the cable to the camera

2 Connect the other end of the cable to the computer. This is usually done with a USB (Universal Serial Bus) connection

3 Turn on the camera

4 Depending on your computer's operating system, it should recognize the type of camera and prepare to download the photos

Using a memory card reader

You can also download photos from a camera to a computer by using a memory card reader, which is a device that can be connected to the computer. The camera's memory card can be inserted into the card reader. Many card readers will work with all of the different types of memory card on the market. To use a memory card reader:

1 Connect the memory card reader to your computer using the cable that should be supplied with the card reader

2 Remove the memory card from the camera

3 Insert the memory card into the card reader

Don't forget

Card readers that can accommodate a variety of memory cards are known as multi card readers. Look for this type of card reader, as they are more versatile.

Don't forget

When a memory card is inserted into a card reader, the computer will usually recognize this and begin the downloading process.

73

4 The card reader will show up as a separate drive on your computer:

Devices with Removable Storage

3½ Floppy (A:)

CD Drive (D:)

DVD Drive (E:)

Card reader (G:)

Downloading with Windows

Once you have connected your camera or card reader to the computer you can download photos onto the computer. If you are using the Windows operating system this can be done with the Scanner and Camera Wizard:

Hot tip

When a camera or a card reader is connected to the computer, the Scanner and Camera Wizard should start automatically.

1 Click Start and select All Programs>Accessories> Scanner and Camera Wizard

2 The Welcome Screen explains about the Wizard and how it works

3 Click Next to move to the next screen of the Wizard

Don't forget

Once a photo has been selected it will have a green tick next to it in its checkbox.

4 The photos contained on the camera or memory card are displayed

5 Click this box next to a photo to select it for downloading

6 Click Next to move to the next
screen of the Wizard

7 The Picture Name and Destination window enables
you to name the picture group and select where it is
to be saved on your computer

8 Enter a
name for
the group of
photos to be
downloaded

75

9 Click here to select a destination on your computer
for the photos

10 Select a current
folder on your
computer or click
the Make New
Folder button to
create a new folder
into which your
photos can be put.
Click OK

Hot tip

It is a good idea to
create a new folder
for each new batch of
photos downloaded.

11 Click Next to move to the next
screen of the Wizard

Next >

...cont'd

12 The photos are copied to the chosen location

Scanner and Camera Wizard

Copying Pictures
Please wait while the wizard copies your pictures.

Location:
d Settings\default\My Documents\Nick\dp_seniors

Picture:
Sunny afternoon 003

Picture progress: 50% complete

Currently copying picture 3 of 14:

To stop copying, click Cancel.

< Back   Next >   Cancel

Beware

Depending on the number of photos and their size, the downloading process can take a few minutes to complete.

13 Once the photos have been downloaded there are various options for publishing photos to the Web, ordering prints or exiting the Wizard

14 To do nothing, click on this button

Don't forget

Instead of choosing to do nothing here, you could choose to use the photos by publishing them to a page on the Web, or ordering prints directly from an online printing service.

Scanner and Camera Wizard

Other Options
You can choose to keep working with your pictures.

Your pictures have been successfully copied to your computer or network.
You can also publish these pictures to a Web site or order prints online.

What do you want to do?

○ Publish these pictures to a Web site
○ Order prints of these pictures from a photo printing Web site
⊙ Nothing. I'm finished working with these pictures

Learn more about working with pictures.

< Back   Next >   Cancel

15 Click Next to move to the final screen of the Wizard

Next >

16 Click on the link here to view your downloaded photos

17 The photos can now be viewed in the same way as any other photos on your computer

Downloading in photo editors

If you do not want to use the Windows operating system to download your photos you can use a photo editing program, such as Photoshop Elements. This has the advantage of saving the photos within the photo editing program's system, which can make it easier to organize your photos at a later date. To download photos with Photoshop Elements:

Don't forget

For more information about Photoshop Elements, see Chapter Eight.

Beware

If you are using a photo editing program this may launch automatically when a camera or card reader is attached. In some cases, it may launch at the same time as the computer's own downloading wizard. Get into the habit of using just one downloading method.

1 If Photoshop Elements is installed on your computer and a camera or a card reader is connected to the computer, the program recognizes this, launches automatically and opens the Downloader window

2 Under the Save Files heading, click the Browse button to navigate to a folder on your computer where you want to save the downloaded photos

3 Click the box next to a photo to uncheck it if you do not want to include it in the downloading process

5/10/2007
DSC_0060.JPG

4 Click the Get Photos button

5 The photos are downloaded from the camera

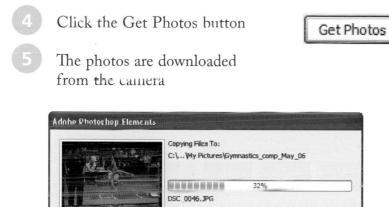

6 The photos are then copied into the Photoshop Elements Organizer area

...cont'd

Beware

Only delete the photos from the memory card if you are sure you are not going to need them on the memory card any more, i.e. you do not want to use it to download onto another computer or obtain prints directly from the card.

7 Once the photos have been downloaded the following window appears to ask whether you now want to delete the photos from the downloading device (the camera or memory card). If you do, click Yes

8 The downloaded photos are displayed on their own in the program's Organizer section

9 Click the Back to All Photos button to view all of the photos that have been downloaded with the program

Back to All Photos

Viewing photos

Once photos have been downloaded onto your computer
(using Windows) they can be viewed in a number of ways:

1 To begin viewing
photos, click the Start
button

2 Select the location
where your photos
have been downloaded.
By default, this will be
My Pictures

3 In the My Pictures window all of the folders
containing photos are displayed. (These folders can
be created when photos are first downloaded)

If you create sub-
folders within the main
picture folders, the
main folder will not
display any thumbnails
(small pictures) of the
items within it. If it
is just a single folder,
thumbnails will be
visible, depending on
the viewing mode.

...cont'd

Don't forget

For more details about creating and viewing slide shows, see Chapter Twelve.

4 Double-click on a folder to open it and view its contents

5 Click here to view the contents of the folder as a slide show

6 Click here for options for viewing the photos in a folder

Picture Tasks
- Get pictures from camera or scanner
- View as a slide show
- Order prints online
- Print pictures
- Copy all items to CD

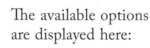
Barcelona2

File Edit View Favorites Tools Help

Back ▾   Search Folders

7 The available options are displayed here:

- Filmstrip
  Thumbnails
  Tiles
  Icons
  List
  Details

8 Select Filmstrip to view thumbnails and larger versions of each photo

9 Select Thumbnails to view small versions of each photo

Don't forget

In Filmstrip view, each photo that is selected as a thumbnail along the bottom strip is displayed at a larger size in the area above.

...cont'd

10 Select Tiles to view icons and file information about each photo

In Tiles view, the filename, photo size and file type are displayed next to the image icon.

11 Select Icons to view an icon of each photo

12 Select List to view all photos in list format

(screenshot of Barcelona2 window in List view)

Hot tip

In all views, if you move the cursor over an item, additional information is displayed about it.

13 Select Details to view a list of all photos, with file details next to them

(screenshot of Barcelona2 window in Details view)

Don't forget

Details view contains the most information about individual files. One particularly useful option is the Date Modified column.

Downloading with a Mac

If you use an Apple Mac computer the downloading process is taken over by the computer, using a program called iPhoto that comes already installed on all new Macs. To download photos with a Mac:

1. Connect the camera or card reader to the computer

2. iPhoto will open automatically and recognize that a digital device has been connected

3. Click the Import button to download the photos

4. Once the photos have been downloaded they are available to view in the iPhoto window

Creating a digital shoebox

When all photos came in printed format it was easy to collect vast numbers of photos that were hardly ever looked at. Drawers and shoeboxes were filled with photos and packed away in cupboards and attics. With the digital age the need for physically storing photos has been greatly reduced. However, our computers have now become the equivalent of the old-fashioned shoebox and it is easy to get hundreds, or thousands, of photos scattered around different locations on your computer. To try and overcome this, and give some order to your digital shoebox, it is worth creating a file structure into which your photos can be saved when they are downloaded. To do this:

1. Click the Start button

2. Select My Pictures

3. The My Pictures window contains everything to create a new file structure

4. Click the "Make a new folder" option under File and Folder Tasks

5. Give the folder a top-level name for a collection of photos, such as Vacations

...cont'd

6 Double-click on the new folder to open it. At this point it will be empty

7 Repeat Steps 4 and 5 to create subfolders of the top-level one. These could be for specific years

8 Keep creating subfolders until you have created a suitable file structure

9 Click on the Folders button to view the complete file structure

 Folders

7 Examining photos

This chapter shows how digital photographs are created and how to resize them to suit the way you want to use them

Dissecting a digital photo

Since digital photographs are made up of a collection of colored building blocks (pixels), there is a great deal of flexibility when it comes to viewing and editing them. Using a photo editing program, you can edit each individual pixel – i.e. change its color – as well as changing large areas of a photograph. By looking at a digital photograph in a photo editing program, you can understand more about how they are created. To do this:

Don't forget

The most common file format for digital photographs is JPEG, which stands for Joint Photograph Experts Group. This is the format in which most digital cameras capture photographs.

1. Open an image in a photo editing program. By default the whole image will be visible

2. At the top of the editing window are details of the file name and the file format (in this case it is a JPEG, denoted by the .jpg extension)

dissecting1.jpg

3. The size at which the image is being viewed is displayed next to the file name

@ 21.1%

4. By increasing the magnification of the image, individual areas can be seen more closely

By increasing the magnification to its full value, individual pixels can be viewed

Don't forget

Photo editing (including viewing images at different sizes) is looked at in more detail in Chapter Eight.

 Photo editing can be used to edit individual pixels in a digital photo

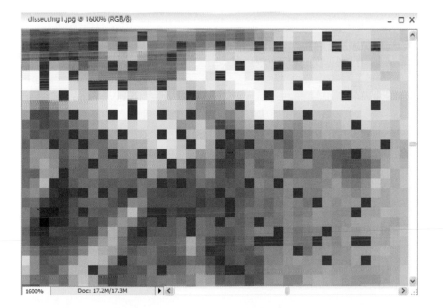

Solving the resolution riddle

In the world of digital photography you will sooner or later (probably sooner) come across the concept of resolution. While this term refers to a number of different aspects of digital photography, the most important one relates to the size of images in terms of pixels (the colored electronic building blocks that make up digital images).

Photo resolution

When looking at a digital camera you will be quoted a headline figure giving the number of pixels it can capture for each photograph. This can either be stated as an overall headline figure, e.g. 8 million pixels (or 8 megapixels), or as the dimensions of an image (e.g. 1800 pixels x 1200 pixels).

Most digital cameras can capture images at various different resolution settings (with different numbers of pixels). A camera's manual will tell you the number of pixels at each setting. This is sometimes referred to as the image size or image dimensions.

The importance of pixels and resolution is that they determine the size at which images can be displayed on a computer monitor and printed to a high quality.

Printed images

Most people want to print at least some of their digital photographs and, as a general rule, for printed images you want as many pixels as possible.

For printed images a setting of 300 pixels per inch (ppi) is used for optimum quality. This means that each linear inch of the printed image will contain 300 pixels. To work out the size of the final printed image that can be printed at high quality, divide the pixel dimensions of the image by 300. So an image with a resolution of 1800 x 1200 would be printable at high quality at 6 inches x 4 inches. If the resolution of the image were lower, i.e. it had fewer pixels, it could still be printed at the same size but the result would be of inferior quality as there would be fewer pixels in each inch of the image.

Beware

The various elements connected with resolution in digital photography can be confusing so it is worth spending a bit of time coming to terms with each one.

The following table illustrates the resolution, in terms of number of pixels, required for various sizes of prints (presuming that they are printed at 300 ppi).

Overall pixels	Dimensions (pixels)	Print size (inches at 300 ppi)
8 million	3264 x 2448	11 x 8 (approx.)
5 million	2592 x 1944	8 x 6 (approx.)
3 million	2048 x 1536	7 x 5 (approx.)
1 million	1280 x 960	4 x 3 (approx.)

When capturing images that you know will be printed, do so with the largest number of pixels possible, i.e. at the highest image size setting on your camera.

Web images

Images on the Web are traditionally displayed at about 72 ppi as this is the resolution of standard computer monitors. This means that in a linear inch of the screen 72 pixels of the digital photo are displayed. Because of this, photos for the Web can be captured at a considerably smaller size, i.e. fewer pixels, than ones that are going to be printed.

Recap

- For photos for printing, use the highest resolution setting on your camera, i.e. the most pixels

- For photos for the Web, use a lower resolution setting

- If in doubt, use the highest resolution setting (photos can be made smaller later with photo editing programs)

- To work out the size of printed photos, divide the pixel dimensions (height and width) of a photo by 300

- To work out the size of online photos, divide the pixel dimensions (height and width) of a photo by 72

Don't forget

When looking at digital cameras remember that the headline figure that is quoted by manufacturers or retailers (e.g. 5 megapixels) is the number of pixels captured at the camera's highest resolution setting.

Making photos smaller

Since digital photographs are made up of individual pixels it is possible to reduce the size of the photos by removing pixels from the original. This has to be done with a photo editing program on a computer. One of the most common reasons for making images smaller is so that they can be viewed at their actual size on a computer without having to scroll around the screen to see the whole photo. To make a photo smaller, using Photoshop Elements:

1 Open a photo in your chosen photo editing program and view it at its actual size, i.e. 100% magnification (depending on the size of the image this may make it larger than the monitor on which it is being viewed, in which case you will only see part of it)

2 Access the Image Size window within the photo editing program. This is usually done from the program's Menu bar by selecting an option similar to Image>Resize>Image Size

3 The Image Size window contains all of the necessary functions for changing the size of the photo

Image Size

Learn more about: <u>Image Size</u>

OK
Cancel
Help

Pixel Dimensions: 4.87M

Width: 1600 | pixels ▾
Height: 1064 | pixels ▾

Document Size:

Width: 13.55 | cm ▾
Height: 9.01 | cm ▾
Resolution: 300 | pixels/inch ▾

☑ Scale Styles
☑ Constrain Proportions
☑ Resample Image: Bicubic ▾

Don't forget

The process of making digital photos smaller or larger is know as resampling. Making photos smaller is known as resampling down and making photos larger is known as resampling up.

95

4 Make sure that the Resample Image and the Constrain Proportions boxes are both checked

☑ Constrain Proportions

☑ Resample Image: Bi

5 The current dimensions (in pixels) of the photo are shown in the Pixel Dimensions section of the Image Size window

Pixel Dimensions: 4.87M

Width: 1600 | pixels ▾
Height: 1064 | pixels ▾

...cont'd

Hot tip

The link symbol connecting the Width and Height boxes appears when the Constrain Proportions box is checked.

6 Enter a lower number in the Width or Height box to make the photo smaller.

Pixel Dimensions: 701.4K (was 4.87M)

Width: 600 pixels
Height: 399 pixels

If the link symbol is showing next to the Width and Height boxes this means that the proportions are constrained, i.e. if you change one value then the other is automatically updated to keep the photo in its original proportions

7 Click OK to apply the changes

OK

8 When viewed at actual size in the photo editing program, the photo now appears smaller, since its physical size, i.e. the number of pixels, has been reduced. This will also reduce the overall file size of the photo

daffodil2_copy.jpg @ 100% (RGB/8)

100%   5.08 cm x 3.38 cm (300 ppi)

Making photos larger

The process for making digital photos larger is similar to that for making them smaller, except that pixels are added rather than removed. The photo editing program adds pixels to the photo through a process of complex digital guesswork known as interpolation. This involves looking at the existing pixels in the photo and then working out the best possible color for new pixels that are added next to the existing ones. Although this sounds a bit hit and miss, it is surprisingly accurate and it can be hard to notice the difference afterwards. The most common use for making photos larger is so that they can be printed at a higher quality and/or larger size. To make a photo larger:

Beware

Making digital photos larger by adding more pixels does result in a slight deterioration in quality, but this is not always noticeable.

1   Open a photo in your chosen photo editing program and view it at its actual size, i.e. 100% magnification (depending on the size of the image this may make it smaller than the editing window)

2   Access the Image Size window within the photo editing program. This is usually done from the program's Menu bar by selecting an option similar to Image>Resize>Image Size

3   Make sure that the Resample Image and Constrain Proportions boxes are checked

☑ Constrain Proportions
☑ Resample Image: Bicubic   ▼

4 The current dimensions (in pixels) of the photo are shown in the Pixel Dimensions section of the Image Size window

Pixel Dimensions: 238.9K

Width: 350 — pixels

Height: 233 — pixels

5 Enter a higher number in the Width or Height box to make the photo larger

Pixel Dimensions: 955.7K (was 238.9K)

Width: 700 — pixels

Height: 466 — pixels

6 Click OK to apply the changes

OK

7 When viewed at actual size in the photo editing program, the photo now appears larger, since its physical size, i.e. the number of pixels, has been increased. This will also increase the overall file size of the photo

fireworks1_copy.jpg @ 100% (RGB/8)

100%   Doc: 955.7K/955.7K

Preparing for printing

If you want to get photos printed by someone else, such as a photographic retail store or an online service, make sure that the photos are captured at the camera's highest available image size, i.e. the one with the most pixels.

If you want to print photos yourself on a home printer it is still important to capture the photos at the highest image size. Once this has been done, you can then use a photo editing program to specify the size and quality at which you want the photos to be printed. To do this:

1. Open a photo in your photo editing program and access the Image Size window within the photo editing program. This is usually done from the program's Menu bar by selecting an option similar to Image>Resize>Image Size

2. The number of pixels in the photo is shown at the top of the Image Size window

> Pixel Dimensions: 9.01M
>
> Width: 2100   pixels
>
> Height: 1500   pixels

3. To retain the current number of pixels, make sure the Resample Image box is not checked

> ☐ Resample Image:

4. The size of the printed photo is determined by the figure in the Resolution box in the Document Size section. In this example this results in a printed image of 7 x 5 inches, i.e. 2100 divided by 300 and 1500 divided by 300

> Document Size:
>
> Width: 7   inches
>
> Height: 5   inches
>
> Resolution: 300   pixels/inch

Don't forget

If a checkbox is not checked then it is empty. If it is checked, a colored tick will appear in the box.

...cont'd

5 If you want to print the photo at a larger size, enter the relevant figures in the Width and Height boxes. In the example, the Width was set to 10 inches, giving a proportional size of 7.143 inches for the Height. This results in a print resolution of 210 pixels per inch, i.e. 2100 divided by 10 and 1500 divided by 7.143

Document Size:

Width: 10 — inches

Height: 7.143 — inches

Resolution: 210 — pixels/inch

Hot tip

Experiment with the various settings in the Image Size window to see how changing one value affects another. This will give you a good understanding of the resizing process for digital photographs.

6 If you want to increase the number of pixels in a photo (in order to retain the document size settings) check the Resample Image box

☑ **Resample Image:**

7 The print resolution of the photo can now be increased without changing the Width and Height sizes

Document Size:

Width: 10 — inches

Height: 7.143 — inches

Resolution: 300 — pixels/inch

8 To accommodate the increase in resolution, the number of pixels in the photo has been increased by the photo editing software

Pixel Dimensions: 18.4M (was 9.01M)

Width: 3000 — pixels

Height: 2143 — pixels

Preparing for the Web

If digital photos are going to be used online, i.e. displayed on a Web page, it is important that the image is not too large, in terms of both file size and pixel dimensions. This is because a large file will take longer to download on a Web page and also because a large photo may take up too much space on the monitor. Most photo editing programs have an option for saving photos for the Web:

1. Select File>Save For Web from the Menu bar

2. The Save For Web window offers several options for saving the photo and reducing its file size and number of pixels

3. The left-hand panel displays the photo and its current settings. The right-hand panel shows details of the photo once the changes have been made

Don't forget

When preparing images for the Web, divide the number of pixels in the Height and Width of the image by 72 to work out the approximate size (in inches) at which it will be viewed on a Web page.

101

...cont'd

4 The Save For
Web window
has options for
the way the
photo is saved.
These include
the file format
and the quality.
A reduction in
the Quality value results in the size of the file being
reduced but it does not always lead to a noticeable
reduction in image quality

Beware

Try not to use the GIF
file format for digital
photographs. This is
because it uses fewer
colors to represent the
photographs, which
can lead to inferior
quality.

102

5 In the Image
Size section of
the Save For
Web window,
the physical size
of the photo
can be changed
by entering
new figures in
the Width and
Height boxes.
This can be
done to ensure
that a photo is
displayed at a smaller size on the Web

6 Click OK to
apply any editing
changes that have
been made

8 Editing photos

Digital photo editing on a computer is a great way to improve elements of photos and also have some fun with them. This chapter offers advice about choosing a program and also shows some common photo editing techniques.

Picking an editing program

Photo editing programs are used on computers to manipulate digital photos. There are a wide variety available and they vary considerably in terms of functions and price. For the examples in this book, Photoshop Elements is used. This is an excellent program in terms of functions, value for money and ease of use and fulfils all of the criteria for a general-use photo editing program. The main functions of Photoshop Elements are:

Editing

Elements provides powerful editing functions, within a clear interface that includes a number of Help options:

Don't forget

For more information about Photoshop Elements, have a look at "Photoshop Elements 4 in Easy Steps" in this series.

The editing functions within Photoshop Elements are presented in a Tools panel that contains the selection tools, crop tool, red-eye removal tool, text tool, coloring tools and cloning tools. There is also a Menu bar that can be used to access common commands and a Toolbar for functions such as opening new files, printing, and accessing other areas of the program such as the Organizer section and the Creation section.

Organizing

A whole area is given over to organizing photos so that they can be easily found and sorted:

Creating

As well as editing and organizing, Elements also has several options for using digital photos, including creating slide shows and creative emails, and even publishing them on your own Web page:

Viewing photos

The first thing that most people want to do with a photo editing program is to look at their photos. Once photos have been opened within a photo editing program, they can then be viewed at different magnifications.

Opening photos

The procedure for opening photos with a photo editing program is virtually the same, regardless of the program. To do this:

 Select File>Open from the Menu bar or click on this button

 Browse to the photos that are on your computer and click on one to select it

Click Open to open the selected photo in the photo editing program

Open

 The photo is opened within the photo editing program, ready for editing

Magnifying images

By default, photos are opened within a photo editing program so that you can see all of them. However, there will be occasions when you will want to zoom in on a particular part of a photo, for editing purposes. There are various ways in which this can be done, but one of the best is by using the Zoom tool. To do this:

Don't forget

When carrying out certain editing functions, such as selecting areas, it can be beneficial to zoom in on the photo to edit parts of it as accurately as possible.

1　Open an image

2　Click here on the Tools panel

107

3　Position the Zoom tool over part of an image. If a plus sign is showing this will zoom in on the photo

4　Click on part of the photo to zoom in on it

5　Press Alt and click on the photo to change the function to zoom out, which is denoted by a minus sign in the Zoom tool

Brightening dull photos

When taking digital photos, sometimes the end result is either slightly too dark or too light. This can be because of the lighting conditions at the time or because of the way that the camera works. Either way, this is not a serious problem because the lighting can be improved within a photo editing program. To do this:

Hot tip

It is usually more effective to lighten dark photos than to darken light ones.

1 Open a photo that looks either too dark or too light

2 Access the Brightness/Contrast command by selecting Enhance>Adjust Lighting>Brightness/Contrast from the Menu bar

3 Drag the sliders for Brightness and Contrast to lighten or darken the image

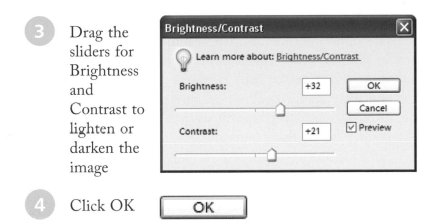

Brightness/Contrast

Learn more about: Brightness/Contrast

Brightness: +32

Contrast: +21

☑ Preview

OK
Cancel

4 Click OK

OK

5 The selected options will be applied to the photo

DSC_0120.JPG @ 25% (RGB/8)

25%   Doc: 9.54M/9.54M

6 Save the photo to keep the changes, by selecting File>Save from the Menu bar

Making photos crisper

One result of taking photos with digital technology is that they are sometimes not as crisp as film photographs and can appear slightly "soft". This is not always apparent with the naked eye but it can be seen in photo editing programs if the photo is magnified. Photo editing programs can also be used to make the image appear crisper, a process known as sharpening. To do this:

1 Open a photo. Initially, it may not look as if it needs to be made crisper

2 Access the Sharpen commands by selecting Filter>Sharpen from the Menu bar

3 Select the Unsharp Mask option

4 The Unsharp Mask window gives options for making the photo crisper

5 Drag the Amount slider to change the level of sharpening

6 The Preview box shows how the level of sharpening affects the photo

Unsharp Mask

OK
Cancel
☑ Preview

─ 100% ＋

Amount: 151 %

Radius: 1.0 pixels

Threshold: 0 levels

7 Click OK

OK

8 The photo now looks much crisper

caddell_apr_06 102.jpg @ 66.7% (RGB/8)   _ □ ✕

66.67%   Doc: 17.2M/17.2M   ▶ ◀   ◀   ▶

Beware

If too much sharpening is applied it can make the photo look unnatural and too jaggy. Therefore, apply sharpening in small amounts and reapply the technique if required.

Using the best parts

With most digital photos there are areas that do not add anything to the photo and in some cases they detract from it. This could be an unwanted background behind a photo of grandchildren or a large area of unwanted sky behind a famous landmark. A technique known as cropping can be used to remove unwanted areas of a photo, leaving just the best parts. To do this:

112

1 Open a photo that has an area of unwanted background

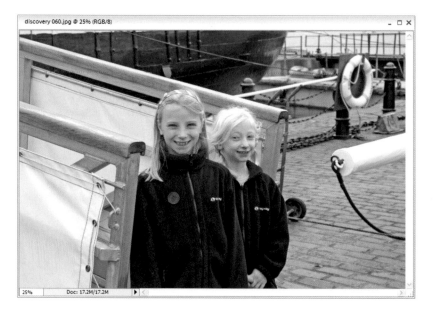

2 The Crop tool is located within the Tools panel

3 Click here to select the Crop tool

Drag around the part of the photo that you want to keep

 Click the tick to apply the cropping changes

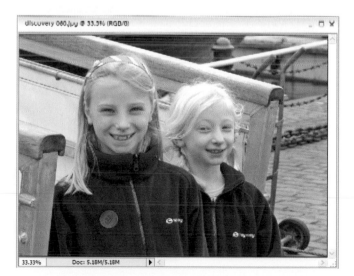 The cropped part is now the whole photo

 Hot tip

Photoshop Elements has a function for constraining the size of the cropped area to certain proportions. This is useful if you want to print the photo at a specific size, e.g. 7 x 5 inches.

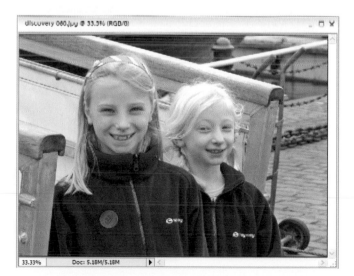

Getting artistic

Photo editing programs have a variety of special effects that can be added to photos. These can be used to create an artistic effect or to make a surreal image from the photo. Effects can be accessed from the Filter menu on the Menu bar or from the Styles and Effects panel. To add artistic effects:

Hot tip

Effects can also be applied by dragging them onto the currently open photo, from the Styles and Effects panel.

1 Open a photo to which you want to add effects

2 Access the Styles and Effects panel by selecting Window>Styles and Effects from the Menu bar

3 Click here to select the different Styles and Effects

4 Double-click a style or effect to apply it to the currently open image

5 Some Styles and Effects have additional windows in which the properties for the style or effect can be set

6 The selected style or effect is applied to the image

Adding messages

Adding messages to digital photos is a great way to personalize photos and give them an extra dimension. This is done by writing on a photo with the Text tool. To do this:

1 Open a photo to which you want to add a message

2 Click here to select the Text tool on the Tools panel

3 Click here to select the font

Verdana

4 Click here to select the size

48 pt

5 Click here to select the color

Color:

6 Click on the photo at the point where you want to start typing

7 Type the message

Don't forget

Make sure that the text is large enough so that it can be read easily on the photo.

8 To move the message, select the Move tool on the Tools panel

9 Click on the text box and drag it to move the message around the photo

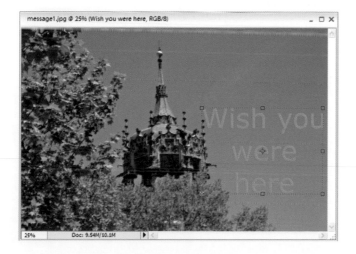

Airbrushing photos

One of the most effective and striking editing techniques for digital photos is airbrushing. This involves removing or altering part of the original photo. This could be to remove blemishes in the photo, or to remove large elements such as people or buildings. Airbrushing is achieved with the Clone tool, which is used to copy one part of the photo over another. To airbrush a photo using the Clone tool:

118

1 Open a photo that contains an item you want to remove

2 Click on the Clone tool on the Tools panel (this is sometimes also known as the Stamp tool)

3 Hold down Alt and click on the part of the photo that you want to use to cover the area to be removed. This serves to load the Clone tool

4 Move the cursor over the part of the photo that you want to airbrush out

Hot tip

Perform the cloning in small steps and release the mouse regularly. This will enable you to undo each step if it has gone wrong, without having to undo the whole process, which would be the only option if you had not released the mouse button.

5 Click and drag over the required element. The area selected in Step 3 is now copied onto the area over which the cursor passes

119

6 Try cloning from different areas to create a smooth background for the cloned area

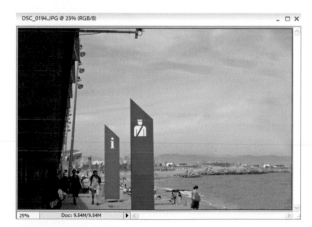

Adding family members

When capturing photos of family groups it is inevitable that one person (or more) is not there at the time. Instead of leaving them out of the final photo, it is possible to use a photo editing program to add them to the original photo. To do this:

 Open a photo of the missing person

Don't forget

Selections can also be made using the Magnetic Lasso tool and the Polygonal Lasso tool.

 Click on the Lasso tool in the Tools panel

Click and drag around the missing person to make a selection. This does not have to be too accurate

Select Edit>Copy from the Menu bar

5 Open the photo of the family group

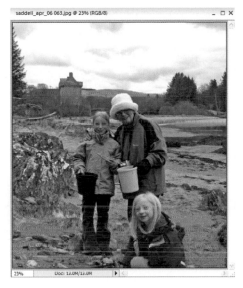

saddell_apr_06 063.jpg @ 23% (RGB/8)

23%   Doc: 13.0M/13.0M

Edit   Image   Enhance

↺ Undo Brightness/C
↻ Redo
↶ Revert

Cut
Copy
Copy Merged
Paste

6 Select Edit>Paste from the Menu bar

7 The copied selection is pasted into the group photo

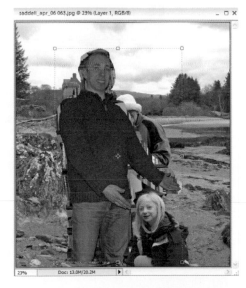

saddell_apr_06 063.jpg @ 23% (Layer 1, RGB/8)

23%   Doc: 13.0M/20.2M

Don't forget

Don't worry if the pasted selection looks too large as it can easily be resized (see next page).

...cont'd

Hot tip

For the greatest accuracy when erasing parts of a photo, zoom in to the maximum magnification (1600%) so that individual pixels can be removed.

 8 Zoom in on the pasted selection and click on the Eraser tool in the Tools panel

 9 Click and drag to remove any unwanted parts of the selection

10 Click on the Move tool

11 Hold down the Shift key and drag on one of the corner markers around the selection. This will enable you to resize it proportionally

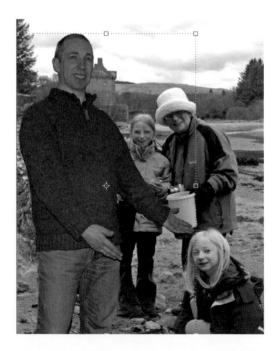

12 Use the Move tool to position the missing person within the complete group

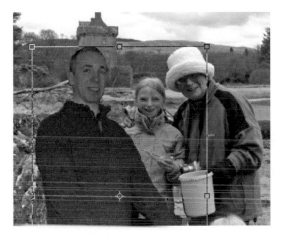

13 General editing techniques can then be applied to the photo, such as editing the overall color

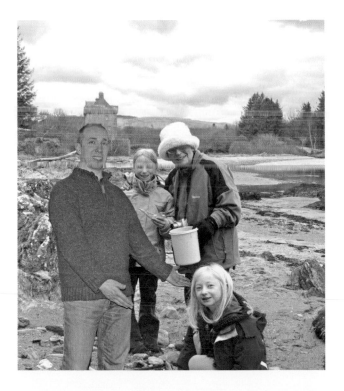

Organizing photos

In addition to being able to edit photos, most photo editing programs have a facility for organizing photos so that you can find them quickly. In Photoshop Elements this is done within the Organizer section of the program. To use this:

 Access the Organizer

 Click Date View to see dates when photos have been downloaded

124

Click Photo Browser to see all of the photos that have been downloaded

Adding tags

Within the Organizer, named tags can be added to photos so that they can be found quickly. To do this:

1 Click on the Tags tab within the Photo Browser

2 Drag a tag onto a photo, or selection of photos

Hot tip

More than one tag can be added to a photo, so that you can later find it by using a variety of criteria.

125

3 Click on the box next to the relevant tag

4 All tagged photos will be displayed

...cont'd

Adding collections

Creating collections of photos is a similar process to adding tags. To do this:

1 Click on the Collections tab within the Photo Browser

2 Select New>New Collection

3 Enter a name for the collection and click OK

4 Drag the collection icon onto a photo, or group of photos

5 Click on the box next to the relevant collection

6 The photos in the collection will be displayed

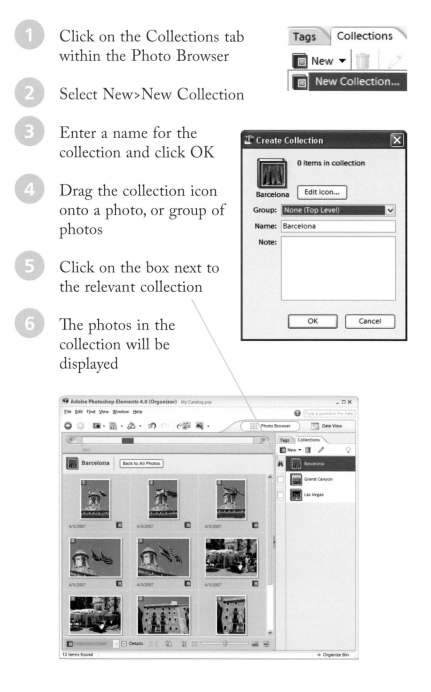

9 Using photos and email

Email is one of the most popular uses for digital photos. It is a quick and cheap way to share your photos with family and friends worldwide.

Getting the right size

Email is one of the most popular uses for digital photos and it is easy to see why:

- It is quick. Photos of family, friends or newborn grandchildren can be distributed around the globe in a matter of minutes from the time they are taken

- It is cheap. Once you have an Internet connection there is no additional cost in sending a photo by email

- It is inclusive. Large numbers of people can be sent the same photos, at the same time

Before looking at the details of sending and receiving photos by email, it is useful to look at the issue of file size. When you are emailing digital photos there are two important considerations:

- Will the photos be viewed in an online environment, i.e. on a computer monitor?

- Will the photos be printed?

This is important because photos for use online can be considerably smaller, in terms of physical size and of file size, than those for printing. There are three ways to make your photos the correct size for the use to which they will be put:

- Set the size when capturing the photo. As shown in Chapter 2, page 30, the picture size can be specified within the camera's menu system. If you know your photo is going to be viewed online you can set the size to a lower setting, e.g. 2 megapixels. Conversely, if you know the photo will be printed out, then select the highest value for the picture size, e.g. 6 megapixels. The larger the picture size the greater the overall file size

- Let your software set the size automatically (see Chapter Seven, page 101 for details) when preparing photos for the Web or email

- Set the size manually with software (see Chapter Seven, pages 94–100 for details)

Sending photos by email

Once you have downloaded your photos and got them ready for sending to family and friends you can then start the process of attaching them to an email. There are two ways in which this can be done:

- Directly from a photo editing program

- By attaching the photo to an email in an email program, such as Outlook or Outlook Express

Sending with a photo editing program

All photo editing programs differ slightly in how they operate, but the process is generally like this:

- You open up a photo in the photo editing program

- Select the Email Photo option

- Select various options for adding text and, in some cases, artistic formatting to the photo

- Send the email with the photo included

To send a photo by email using Photoshop Elements:

Don't forget

Sending a photo with a photo editing program gives you more scope for creating an artistic design and appearance.

129

1 Access the Organizer area and select a photo

2 Select Share>E-mail from the toolbar

...cont'd

 The Attach Email dialog window has various options for formatting the photo email

Attach Selected Items to E-mail

Items

Select Recipients
☑ Vandome, Nick

Choose Format
Format: Photo Mail (HTML) ▾

Select Settings
☑ Include Captions
Estimated Size: ~73.00 KB, 25 sec @ 56Kbps

Message
Here are the photos that I want to share with you.

⊕ Add

Edit Contacts...

Next   Cancel   Help

Hot tip

Photos can be sent to multiple recipients at the same time simply by adding their email addresses to the message.

4 Check this box to select an email recipient

Select Recipients

☑ Vandome, Nick

5 Click here to access the Contact Book to add more addresses for email contacts

Edit Contacts...

6 Click here to select the format for the email

Choose Format

Format: Photo Mail (HTML) ▾

7 Enter the message for the email. This will appear in the body of the email

---

Message

Here are the photos that I want to share with you.

---

8 Click Next to move to the next step of the process

9 Select the formatting options for the email. This gives the photo email a more designed look

Don't forget

As well as formatting the design, you can also add formatted text to the photo email message.

10 Click Next Step to move to the next step of the process

...cont'd

11 Click here for more formatting and click Next

12 Your email program will open automatically, with the formatted photo email already prepared

13 Click Send to send the email

Sending with an email program

1 Open your email program and click here to create a new, blank email

Create Mail

2 The email opens but with no content

Hot tip

If you are unsure about the speed of the recipient's Internet connection, send them a text email first and tell them the file size of the photo you want to send them.

133

3 Click here and select a recipient from your email address book

4 Enter a subject for the email in the Subject box

5 Enter text for the email

6 Click here to attach a photo

Attach

Hot tip

Attach the photo before you enter the text for the email. This way you will not be in danger of forgetting to add the photo and sending the email without it.

...cont'd

Hot tip

Numerous photos can be attached to a single email. To select more than one photo, hold down Ctrl when you click on the photos in Step 7.

7 Browse your hard drive to the location of the photo that you want to attach

8 Select the photo you want and click Attach

9 Details of the photo (including its file size) appear in the Attach box that is now included in the header of the email

To: nickvandome@mac.com

Cc:

Subject: Sending photos

Attach: botanics_2005 016.jpg (2.74 MB)

10 Click Send to send the email in the normal way

Send

Receiving photos by email

When receiving photos by email you will not usually have prior warning. However, if you know that someone is going to be sending you a photo or, more importantly, several photos, it can be a good idea to ask the person to make sure that the file size is not too large. This is because emails with very large attachments (say, over 5 megabytes) can sometimes be stopped by email servers or they can take a long time to download, particularly if a dial-up connection is being used. If you have been sent a photo in an email the following will happen:

1. Open your email program. If it does not start downloading automatically, click on the Send/Receive button

2. The download box appears if there is a message to receive and shows how long the download is taking

3. Once the download is complete the email is displayed, together with the photo attachment

Don't forget

When an email is being downloaded you have no idea whether it contains a photo as an attachment or not. However, if it is taking a few minutes to download then it almost certainly has some type of attachment.

135

Viewing photos from email

Once you have received a photo in an email there are two ways in which it can be viewed, without saving it first:

Viewing within an email

Depending on the type of email program, the photo can be viewed directly within the body of the email:

1 Open the email

Don't forget

The presence of an attachment should be noted in the Attach box at the heading of the email. If this is not visible, it probably means that the sender has forgotten to attach the photo before sending the message.

2 If the photo is not visible, scroll down the window until the photo comes into view

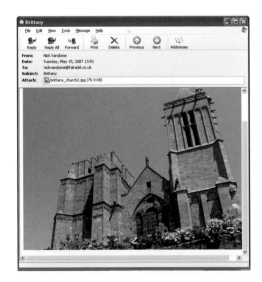

Opening from an email

It is possible to open a photo directly from an email:

1 Double-click on the photo icon in the Attach box

2 A warning dialog window appears

3 Click on the "Open it" button

4 Click OK

5 The photo will be opened in your default photo editing program. At this point the photo will not be saved

Saving photos from email

When you receive a photo in an email you will probably want to save it to your hard drive, or an external device, so that you can view the photo at any time and manipulate it if required. There are two ways to do this:

Within the email

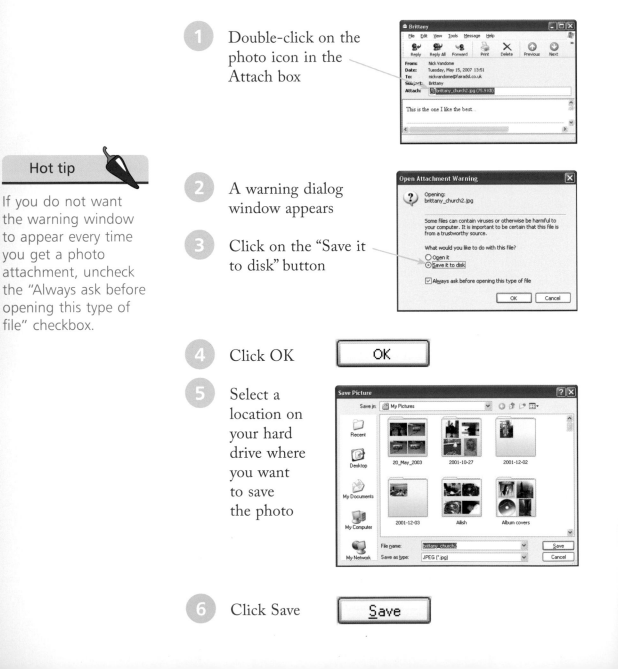

1 Double-click on the photo icon in the Attach box

2 A warning dialog window appears

3 Click on the "Save it to disk" button

4 Click OK

5 Select a location on your hard drive where you want to save the photo

6 Click Save

... cont'd

From the Menu bar

Photo attachments can also be saved by using commands from the Menu bar. To do this:

1 Open the email with the photo attachment

2 Select File>Save Attachments from the Menu bar

3 The Save Attachments dialog window has options for saving the photo attachment

4 The current attachment is shown here

5 Click here to navigate to a location on your hard drive where you want to save the attachment. Select a folder and click OK

6 Click Save to save the photo attachment to the destination selected in Step 5

Printing photos from email

A lot of people want to print out photos that they have been sent by email. One way to do this is to save the photo to your own computer and then open it in a photo editing program and access the print command. However, the photo can also be printed directly from the email. To do this (for Windows users):

140

1. Open the email containing the photo attachment and click on the Print icon on the toolbar, or select File>Print from the Menu bar

Print

2. In the Print dialog box, select the printer you want to use. This should be a color printer and preferably a photo-quality one

3. Click on the Preferences button to access the settings for the selected printer

Preferences

Find Printer...

4 Apply the settings in the same way as you would for printing a photo from your own hard drive

Don't forget

Different makes of printers have their own Settings windows, but most of them are similar in allowing the user to select the quality, paper size and paper type.

5 Click on the Show Settings button to check the settings you have selected

Hot tip

Always check the printer settings before you print a photo, particularly if you are intending to print it at the highest quality.

Current Setting

- Best Photo
- **Paper Source**: Sheet
- **Paper Type**: Premium Glossy Phot...
- **Quality**: Best Photo
- **Document Size**: A4 210 x 297 mm
- **Orientation**: Portrait

6 Click Close to close the Settings box

Close

7 Click OK to send the photo to the printer

OK

Creating email groups

When you are sending photos by email there will be many occasions when you want to send a photo to a particular group of people, for instance after a family event such as a wedding or a party. The quickest way to do this is to set up an email group. The photo can then be sent to the group instead of having to send it to people individually. To create an email group:

Don't forget

New members can be added to an existing email group at any time, even if they were not included initially.

Beware

When sending a photo to an email group, double-check to make sure that you really do want to send the photo to all of the people in the group.

1 Open your email program and click on the Addresses button to access the Address Book

2 In the Address Book dialog window, click on the New button and select New Group

3 Enter the name of the group here

4 Click here to add people to your group

5 Click OK once the group has been created

6 The group is denoted by this icon in your Address Book

10 Sharing on the Web

Online sharing services are a way to share photos on the Web with chosen people. This chapter shows how to use them.

How to share photos

Online photo sharing services now proliferate on the Web and it is easy to see why: they offer a wide range of services for sharing and printing photos; they are secure and good value; and they can be accessed directly from your own computer. Once you have joined a photo sharing site, you can also access it from any computer that is connected to the Internet.

Using a photo sharing site is just a question of accessing a website. There are dozens of different photo sharing sites but the processes for using them are virtually identical:

- Once you have found a site that you want to use, you have to register. However, this is free and usually only involves giving your name, an email address and a password

- Once you are registered you can start using the site. The first step is to create individual albums into which you can save your photos. Different albums can be created for a variety of topics

- After an album has been created it can be shared with other people. This is done by sending them an email inviting them to view your photos. Only people you have invited can view your online photo albums. It is usually free to share photos on an online site; if you are ever asked for a fee just for sharing photos, look for another site

- Photos in albums can also be used for online printing. Almost all online sharing services also have a facility for producing prints from your photos and sending them to you. This is one of the ways in which the sites make their money and they always try to promote this side of their service

- Online sharing sites also have a wide range of other merchandise onto which you can put your photos. This includes cards, calendars, jigsaws, mugs, T-shirts and even bags and cushions

Getting registered

Unlike a lot of commercial online services, registering for an online sharing service is quick and easy and is not something that anyone should worry about. Registration is free and there is no obligation to spend any money, unless you want to buy some of the site's products. Remember, the photo sharing part of the site should be free. For all photo sharing sites the registration process is virtually the same:

1 Access the site and click on the Register or Register Now button (on some sites the registration boxes are directly on the homepage)

2 Enter your name, email address and password

3 Click the Create Account button to complete registration

4 Once you have registered you will be taken to your own secure homepage within the site. This is where you can start creating albums and sharing photos

When registering for an online sharing service, give them an online email address (such as Hotmail) if you have one. This is because they will send you a lot of marketing email in an effort to persuade you to use other services

Assessing online services

There are dozens of online sharing services on the Web and which one you choose may just be down to personal taste and the first impression when you look at the homepage. However, some areas to look at include:

- The range of services offered

- Any restrictions on the number of photos you can store and share

- The price for online prints and merchandise

A few online sharing service to consider are:

Shutterfly at www.shutterfly.com

Hot tip

More online sites can be found by entering "online sharing" into a search engine such as Google.

146

Don't forget

UK sites include:

PhotoBox at
www.photobox.co.uk

Snapfish at
www.snapfish.co.uk

Photodeal at
www.photodeal.co.uk

Kodak at
www.kodakgallery.co.uk

Snapfish at www.snapfish.com

ClubPhoto at www.clubphoto.com

Kodak at www.kodakgallery.com

Creating albums

Once you have chosen a photo sharing site and registered, the first thing to do is to create your own albums into which you can copy photos from your own computer, before you start sharing them. To do this:

148

1 Click on the Create New Album icon

My albums
Choose an album to view

Create
New Album

2 The options for creating the album are displayed

View & Edit Photos   Share Photos   Upload Photos

Create or choose an album

Upload photos to a new album.

Album title: My New Album

Album date: November ☑ 11 ☑ 2006 ☑

Description:

Picture title ☐ Use filenames as photo titles.
Continue ▶

3 Enter the details for the album, such as the name and the date on which it was created

Upload photos to a new album.

Album title: Grand Canyon

Album date: November ☑ 11 ☑ 2006 ☑

Description: Trip to Las Vegas and the Grand Canyon

4 Click Continue to move to the next step

5 Options for uploading photos into your album (from your own computer) are displayed

Upload photos to your album

Grand Canyon

Click Browse to select up to 60 JPEG images (.jpg, .jpeg or .jpe) from your computer.

Browse...   Start Uploading

Hot tip

Some sites have a Quick Upload option where the contents of a whole folder can be uploaded, without having to select the photos individually.

6 Click the Browse button to navigate to photos on your own computer

Browse...

7 Select a photo that you want to upload into your online album

8 Click Open

...cont'd

9 Repeat the selection process until you have selected all of the photos that you want to include

Pictures selected: 5	
▦ vegas 211.jpg	Remove
▦ vegas 083.jpg	Remove
▦ vegas 136.jpg	Remove
▦ vegas 225.jpg	Remove
▦ vegas 108.jpg	Remove

10 Click the Start Uploading button to start uploading the photos

11 As the photos are being uploaded an information window tells you what is happening.

Upload photos to your album

Uploading...
Please wait until the upload is completed.

Pictures selected: 5	
▦ vegas 211.jpg	Remove
▦ vegas 083.jpg	Remove
▦ vegas 136.jpg	Remove
▦ vegas 225.jpg	Remove
▦ vegas 108.jpg	Remove

The uploading can take a few minutes, depending on the speed of the Internet connection being used and the number and size of the photos

Don't forget

Individual photos and whole albums can be edited or deleted after they have been created.

12 Once the uploading has been completed, the selected photos are visible in the newly created album

Sharing photos

When photos have been uploaded into an album on the online sharing site, it is then possible to make this album visible to anyone you want, e.g. members of your family and close friends. To do this:

1 Click on the Share Photos tab at the top of your homepage within the online sharing site

2 The page displays the albums that you have created. These are the ones that you can now share with others

Beware

On some sharing sites, people will have to register to view photos once they have been invited. This is the same registration process as for joining the site in the first place.

151

3 Click the Select Album button to select an album for sharing

...cont'd

4 The selected album will be marked as ready to be shared

 2006 Albums

 Grand Canyon
11/11/06 (5 photos)
✓ This album will be shared

5 Click the Continue button to move to the next step

Continue ▶

On some sites you can send a copy of the invitation to yourself, to check that it has been sent.

6 Enter the details of the person, or people, with whom you want to share the album. This includes their email address and a message to go in the accompanying email

Invite your friends to view this slideshow

To: eilidhvandome@mac.com

Separate addresses with commas or semicolons or select addresses from Friends & Groups.

Subject: View my photos from the Grand Canyon

Message: You're invited to view my online photos at the Gallery. Enjoy!

838 characters left

☐ Require friends to sign in to view and save your photos.

Don't forget

Albums and photos are only visible to specific people you have invited.

7 Click the Send Invitation button to invite the selected person, or people, to view your album

Send invitation

8 Confirmation appears that the album has been shared

Your album has been shared

You'll soon receive a copy of the email that was sent to your friends.
Please visit your guestbook to see who has viewed your album and left comments.

View slideshow

➋ Share this slideshow again
➋ Create a new share

Being invited

As well as inviting other people to view your online photo albums you may be invited to view albums that other people have created. If this happens, the process for viewing them is as follows:

1 Open your email program and double-click on the email that you received that invites you to view someone's photos online

153

2 The email will contain details about the invitation to view the photos

Nick has shared photos with you.

You're invited to view my online photos at the Gallery. Enjoy!

– Nick

View photos

Grand Canyon
(1 album)

3 Click the View Photos button   **View photos**

...cont'd

4 Select the type of Internet connection you are using. This will enable the site to optimize the process for your connection

Kodak EasyShare Gallery
United States [Change]

Nick has shared photos with you.

Nick's slideshow
(1 album)

○ Broadband - larger photos, more features
○ Dial-up - faster download per photo

5 Click the View Photos button

6 The photos in the album are displayed in a slide-show format

Don't forget

On some sharing sites, you can change some of the settings for the way the slide show appears, such as accompanying music and background color.

7 Use the control buttons to move through the slide show

11 Getting prints

This chapter details the options for printing digital photos at home, in store or online

Options for printing

In the early days of consumer digital photography, obtaining good quality prints was a considerable issue. The price was relatively high and the quality relatively poor. However, this has changed dramatically, to the point where it is now possible to get excellent quality prints, at good value, from a variety of sources. The main ways are:

- Printing at home. This can be done with a photo-quality inkjet printer. These are inexpensive and can give very good results. Their one drawback is that the price of the ink for these printers can be high, but you only print the photos that you want

- Retail stores. Most consumer photographic retailers now have facilities for printing digital photos, from memory cards, CDs or most removable storage devices. The quality can be comparable to that of film prints and, as you can select which photos are to be printed, the cost is very competitive. You can get your photos in a variety of sizes, up to poster size, and it is also sometimes possible to get photos printed onto items such as T-shirts, mugs and even cakes

- Online printing services. The development of digital photography has resulted in a corresponding growth in online printing services. To use these, you send the photos via the Web to the online service provider, who then prints the photos and sends them back via traditional mail. Again, this provides excellent quality prints and it is a great way to get hard copies without having to leave the comfort of your own home

- Photo printers. One printing innovation in recent years has been photo printers. These are printers that can print photos directly from a memory card or from the camera, without the photos having to be downloaded onto a computer first. Some also have the facility to crop photos and adjust color and red-eye before they are printed. These devices are either inkjet printers or a type called dye-sublimation printers

Printing photos at home

In some ways, printing photos at home on a photo-quality inkjet printer gives you the most flexibility: you can edit the photos on your computer first and then print them out at a specific size. There are two ways in which photos can be printed on a home photo-quality inkjet printer:

Using the operating system

If you are using Windows, photos can be printed directly, without having to open them first. To do this:

1 Access My Pictures, navigate to the required folder of photos and click on one photo to select it

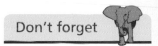
Don't forget

If you are using a Mac, photos can be printed directly from within the iPhoto program or from the Finder.

157

2 Click on the Print this Picture link under Picture Tasks

...cont'd

3 The Photo Printing Wizard appears. This will guide you through the printing process

4 Click the Next button to move to the next step

Next >

5 Select the photos you want to print by clicking on the checkbox next to them. The ones that are selected will have a green tick in the checkbox

6 Click the Next button to move to the next step

Next >

7 Select the printer that you want to use to print the photos

Printing Options
Select the printer and paper you want to use.

What printer do you want to use?

EPSON Stylus Photo R800 | Install Printer...

Your prints will look best if you select the correct paper before printing. To select paper, click Printing Preferences.

Printing Preferences

Currently selected paper: Plain Paper

< Back | Next > | Cancel

Hot tip

Photo-quality color printers give the best results when printing color photos.

8 Click the Printing Preferences button to specify settings for the way the photos will be printed

Printing Preferences

9 The printer properties dialog box has several settings such as print quality and paper type. Both of these are very important when printing digital photos

EPSON Stylus Photo R800 Properties

Main | Page Layout | Maintenance

Quality Option

Draft | Text | Text & Image | Photo | Best Photo

Paper Options

Source: Sheet | Borderless

Type: Plain Paper

Size: A4 210 x 297 mm

Ink Levels

Print Options

Photo Enhance
Gloss
Reverse Order
Print Preview

Orientation

Portrait
Landscape

Show Settings

Reset Defaults | Technical Support | Advanced

OK | Cancel | Help

Hot tip

If you want a draft version of a photo, use a lower quality setting in order to save ink. There is also usually an option for printing the photo in black and white, useful if you just want to get a general impression of how it will look.

10 Select the Best Photo button to ensure that the photo is printed at the printer's highest quality

Best Photo

...cont'd

Hot tip

Buy photo-quality
paper in bulk if you
can, as this will work
out cheaper in the
long run.

11 Select the required paper type. For digital photos, the
heavier the better

12 Click the Next button to move
to the next step

Next >

13 Further options
for the layout
of the printed
photo can also
be selected

14 Click the Next button to move
to the next step

Next >

15 A confirmation
window appears once
the photo has been
printed

16 Click the Finish
button to close the Wizard

Finish

Using photo editing software

Another option for printing photos from your own computer is to use a photo editing program. This can give you more flexibility as far as the formatting of the photo is concerned. To do this, using Photoshop Elements:

1 Access the Organizer section, select a photo and select File>Print from the Menu bar

Don't forget

Printing with a photo editing program enables you to be more creative with the way in which photos are arranged and printed.

161

2 The Print dialog window has various options for how the photo is printed

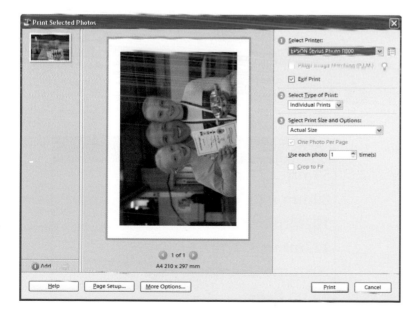

...cont'd

③ Click the Add button to add photos to the current print job. This can enable more than one photo to be printed on a single sheet of paper

④ Select an option for the way the photo (or photos) will be printed. You can choose an individual photo, a contact sheet containing thumbnails of a lot of photos, a Picture Package – which offers options for the way the photo (or photos) will be positioned – or as photo labels

162

⑤ Select the size at which you want the photo to be printed

③ Select Print Size and Options:

Actual Size

Actual Size
53mm x 71mm
89mm x 127mm
102mm x 152mm
127mm x 178mm
203mm x 254mm
Fit on Page
Custom... 88.90mm x 127.00mm

6 Enter the number of copies

Use each photo | 1 | ⬍ | time(s)

7 Select the printer to use. Click here to access the printer preferences

1 **S̲elect Printer:**

EPSON Stylus Photo R800

8 Select the required printer preferences such as quality of print and type of paper

Beware

Always make sure that there is enough ink in your printer before you start a new print job.

163

9 Click OK

OK

10 Click Print to send the job to the printer

Print

In-store printing

A lot of photographic retail stores now have photo kiosks which can be used to select photos and send them for printing. These kiosks can be used in a self-service way, or shop assistants will be happy to offer advice and help with using the kiosks. To print photos from a photo kiosk in a retail store:

1   Insert the media on which the photos are stored into the photo kiosk (this can be the camera's memory card, a CD, a floppy disk or a removable pen drive)

2   Select the photos that you want printed

3   Select the number of prints for each photo (there is no limit to the number of copies that can be made from a photo)

4   Select the size of print

5   Send the photos to the printer

6   The photos will then be printed and delivered, just like prints from a film

Printing photos online

Online printing services are an excellent way to get good value, good quality prints without having to move away from your computer. There are dozens of these services available and they can either be accessed directly on the Web (try entering "online printing" into Google) or, for Windows users, from a link within Windows. Either way, you will have to register for the online site before you can start ordering prints (see Chapter Ten, page 145, for details of registering for an online sharing/printing service). To order prints from an online service:

(see Chapter Ten, page 145,

Don't forget

For Mac users, prints can be ordered online using the iPhoto program.

 Access your chosen online printing site and log in

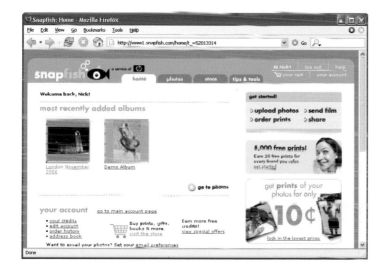

Hot tip

It is free to register for an online printing service and in some cases you get a number of free prints when you register.

2 Click the Order Prints link

...cont'd

Don't forget

See Chapter Ten, page 148, to learn how to create an album on the site.

3 Select an existing album within your site

order prints

Click on the album containing the photos you'd like to order, then click on 'open this album'. <u>Need help?</u>

your albums

⊙ London November 2006

4 Click the Open This Album button

open this album

5 The photos within the album are displayed

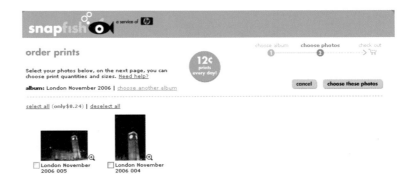

order prints

Select your photos below, on the next page, you can choose print quantities and sizes. <u>Need help?</u>

album: London November 2006 | <u>choose another album</u>

<u>select all</u> (only $0.24) | <u>deselect all</u>

choose album   choose photos   check out

cancel   choose these photos

☐ London November 2006 005   ☐ London November 2006 004

6 Click on the checkbox next to a photo to select it for printing

<u>select all</u> (**only$0.24**) | <u>deselect all</u>

☑ London November 2006 005

☑ London November 2006 004

167

7 Click the Choose These Photos button

choose these photos

8 On the order page, make selections for each photo. These can include the number of copies and the size at which you want the photos printed

quick order

▶▶▶▶▶ 4x6 : 1 ▼ 5x7 : 0 ▼ 8x10 : 0 ▼

	QTY	SIZE	MAIL ORDER PRICES
	1	4x6 (s)	0.12
	0	5x7 (s)	0
	0	8x10 (s)	0
	0	wallet set(s)	0
<u>remove photo</u>		<u>poster prints</u>	

9 Once you have made your selections, click the Check Out button to proceed to the standard online checkout pages to pay for your order

 check out

...cont'd

Ordering from within Windows

Within Windows it is possible to order prints of digital photos without having to first log in to an online sharing and printing service. To do this:

1 Click the Start button and select My Pictures

2 Select a folder containing photos that you want to print

3 Under Picture Tasks, click on the Order Prints Online link

4 The Online Print Ordering Wizard opens. This will guide you through the online printing process

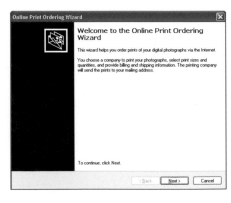

5 Click the Next button to move to the next step

Don't forget
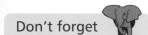

The online services accessed through Windows will vary according to location. However, most online printing sites offer a similar type of service.

168

6 Select the photos that you want to have printed. The selected ones will have a green tick in the checkbox next to them

7 Click the Next button to move to the next step

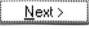

8 Select an online printing service from the options available

9 Click the Next button to move to the next step

10 The software accesses the online service and you can now order prints as you would from an online printing and sharing service

Printing without a computer

Although home printing on an inkjet printer is a flexible and feasible option it is not ideal for everyone, particularly those who are not comfortable working with downloading and editing photos on a computer. One way around this is to use a self-contained photo printer. These are printers that can print photos directly from the camera's memory card or the camera itself, without the need to first download the photos onto a computer. There are two main types of photo printers:

Inkjets

These are inkjet printers that can have memory cards inserted directly into them. Most printers of this type will be able to use all of the different types of memory card on the market, so you do not have to worry about buying a camera with a specific type of memory card.

There is usually a facility for some limited editing, such as cropping and color adjustment, and then the photos can be printed directly from the memory card. In general, inkjet photo printers are more expensive than those that do not offer the facility of printing directly from a memory card. These printers should not be confused with photo-quality inkjet printers, which print photos directly from a computer.

Dedicated camera printers

These are printers that connect directly to the camera (usually by the camera sitting on top of the printer as it would on a docking station – see page 24); the photos can be downloaded directly to the printer. The photos are printed using a method of dye-sublimation which puts a continuous coating of ink on the paper as opposed to the individual dots that are used with an inkjet printer. This produces a very good quality of print but the maximum size is usually restricted to 6 inches by 4 inches.

A lot of manufacturers, such as Kodak, Canon and Sony, have their own dedicated printers that work with their respective brands of cameras.

12 Displaying and keeping

Everyone loves looking at digital photos. This chapter shows some creative ways in which photos can be displayed and also how they can be stored.

Preparing family slide shows

One of the most satisfying aspects of digital photographs is being able to display them to family and friends. One way of doing this is to create slide shows that can then be viewed on a computer or a television. This can be done in two ways:

Within Windows

For Windows users, slide shows can be created within the Windows operating system. However, these can only be viewed on the computer. To do this:

1 Click the Start button and select My Pictures

2 Double-click on a folder in My Pictures to open it

Don't forget

If required, a folder can be selected and then viewed as a slide show. This will automatically display all of the photos in that folder.

3 If desired, select individual photos to include in the slide show. If none are selected, all of the photos will be included

4 Under Picture Tasks, click the "View as a slide show" link

Hot tip

Slide shows such as the one on this page can be displayed on a television, but only if the computer is first connected to it.

5 All of the selected photos are displayed as a slide show

173

...cont'd

Using a photo editing program

In some ways, a better option is to create a slide show with a photo editing program. The advantage of this is that it can be saved as a self-contained presentation and then copied onto a CD so that it can be viewed in more comfort on a television, rather than just on a computer. To do this, using Photoshop Elements:

1 In the Organizer, select the photos you want to use in the slide show

2 Click here to access the Creations part of the program

3 Click here to access the slide show option

4 Select settings for the slide show and click OK

Slide Show Preferences

Slide Show Default Options

Static Duration:	5 sec
Transition:	Fade
Transition Duration:	2 sec
Background Color:	■

☐ Apply Pan & Zoom to All Slides
☑ Include Photo Captions as Text
☑ Include Audio Captions as Narration
☑ Repeat Soundtrack Until Last Slide

Crop to Fit Slide: ☐ Landscape Photos ☐ Portrait Photos

Preview Playback Options

Preview Quality: Medium

☑ Show this dialog each time a new Slide Show is created.

OK   Cancel

Background music can be added to a slide show to give it an extra dimension.

5 Click here to add photos, video or audio to the slide show

Don't forget

Slide shows are automatically created with transitions between each photo, to give them a more professional look.

6 Items in the slide show are displayed here on the timeline

...cont'd

Beware

Use animations sparingly, as a little goes a long way.

7 Click and drag a cartoon figure to add it to an element within the slide show

8 Click here to edit the transitions between elements of the slide show

9 Click here to save the slide show as a specific project file. This will create one self-contained file

Save Project...

10 Give your slide show a name and click Save

Adobe Photoshop Elements

Saving your slide show project enables you to make changes to this slide show later. Your slide show project will be saved to the Photo Browser with today's date. You may need to clear your current search in order to see it.

Name: Edinburgh

Save   Cancel

Saving family slide shows

Once a slide show has been created it can then be saved onto a CD so that it can be displayed on another computer or a television. To save it onto a CD, using Photoshop Elements:

1 Select a slide show that has already been created as shown on the previous three pages

2/5/2007

2 Click here to create a VCD, which is a digital file saved onto a CD

3 Click here to add slide shows. Several slide shows can be added to a single VCD

177

Don't forget

A VCD is created on a CD and offers a quality just below that of a DVD. Once it has been created it can be played on a computer or a DVD player.

Beware

VCDs generally hold about 700 megabytes of data, so keep an eye on the file sizes of the slide shows.

Don't forget

The process of copying information onto a CD, or a DVD, is known as burning.

Hot tip

Different regions around the world use different video formats for files on a VCD (or a DVD). Select the format for the region in which the disc is going to be viewed.

Don't forget

For a VCD, a slide show is considered in the same way as a video file would be.

④ The slide shows to be used on the VCD are displayed here

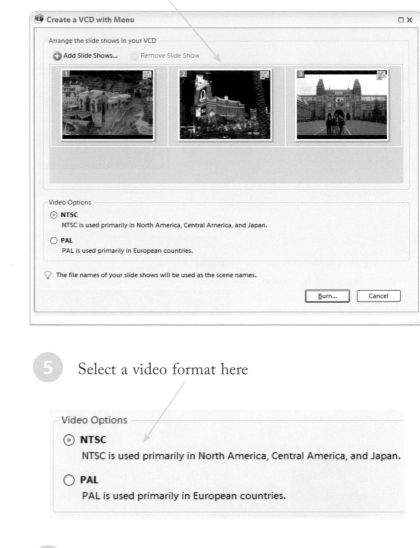

⑤ Select a video format here

Video Options

⊙ **NTSC**
   NTSC is used primarily in North America, Central America, and Japan.

○ **PAL**
   PAL is used primarily in European countries.

⑥ Click Burn to copy the files onto a CD, using your computer's CD writer

Burn...

Viewing from a CD or DVD

In the digital world, digital photographs are frequently saved onto CDs or DVDs. This is an efficient and secure way of saving photos and it also means that photos can easily be transferred from one computer to another. If you are given a CD or DVD containing photos the essential thing is to be able to view them. To do this:

1 Place the CD or DVD in the appropriate drive in the computer

2 The computer should recognize the disc and offer options for viewing. Select an option, such as "View a slideshow of the images," and click OK

Don't forget

When a CD or a DVD has been inserted, the other options for using it include printing the photos directly and also saving them onto your computer.

179

3 If the disc dialog box does not launch automatically click Start and then My Computer. The disc will be shown as a separate drive. Double-click on the disc to open it

4 The contents of the disc are displayed within the normal interface and the photos can be viewed in the usual way

Digital cards

Using a photo editing program such as Photoshop Elements it is possible to produce digital greetings cards or postcards. These can then be printed or sent to people electronically by email. To do this:

1. Access the Creation section and select one of the card-making options

2. There are several options for creating cards, based on a number of templates

3. Click Next Step

4 Click the Add Photos button to add a photo to the card

5 Check the box next to a photo to select it

6 Click the Add Selected Photos button

Add Selected Photos

7 The photo is added to the card template

8 Click Next Step to move to the page where the card can be saved

Next Step >

Creating photo calendars

A personalized calendar makes a great present for family members, and with a photo editing program such as Photoshop Elements it is possible to create them using your own photos. To do this:

Hot tip

Personalized calendars are great Christmas presents, but make sure you create them in plenty of time and with dates for the following year.

1 Access the Creation section. Click here and click OK

2 Click here to select a style for the calendar

3 Select the options for the date format of the calendar and click Next Step

Options

Include: ☑ Title Page   ☑ Captions

Starting: January ⌄ 2007 ⌄   Ending: December ⌄ 2007 ⌄

4 Click here to add photos for the calendar

Don't forget

Use thirteen photos when creating a calendar: one for each month and one for the front cover.

5 Click Next Step

Next Step >

6 Double-click here to add text for the cover page of the calendar

Double-Click to Insert Title

7 Click Next Step

Next Step >

8 Enter a title for the calendar creation. Click Save and then click Done

> You can now save your creation to edit it later.
>
> Calendar Pages **N**ame:
>
> Barcelona
>
> ☐ Use **T**itle for Name

9 Once the calendar is completed it can be printed, sent to someone via email or saved as a PDF file:

The value of backing up

Backing up is the process of creating a copy of your important files so that they are safe in the event of a major accident occurring to your computer, such as fire or theft. If you do not have a backup of your files they could be lost permanently – including your precious photos. Backing up should be seen as general housekeeping and be done as regularly as possible, approximately once every couple of weeks. Some points to bear in mind about backing up:

- It is a chore, but one that could be invaluable. It is a bit like paying for insurance: you hope you never have to use it, but if you do, you are glad you went to the effort

- Back up your files onto some form of removable storage such as a CD or a DVD (external hard drives can be used but they are not as secure because they will probably be located near to the computer – see below). Pen drives are another option for backing up digital photos

- Store your backup copies away from the computer from which they came – if there is an accident such as a fire, you do not want your backups perishing in the same way as the computer. If possible, keep your backups in a separate physical location from the computer

- Some companies on the Web offer online storage where you upload your photos onto their servers, where the photos are stored. However, there is usually a fee for this and there can be issues if the company goes bust or has problems with their servers

- Get into the habit of backing up regularly, particularly after you have downloaded new photos onto your computer. Ideally, enter a recurring reminder into a calendar on your computer

- Always expect the worst – then it will probably never happen, but if it does you will be prepared and hopefully your photos will be preserved

Burning CDs and DVDs

There are programs for saving files to CD or DVD, but this can also be done directly within Windows. To do this:

1 Open My Pictures and select a folder that you want to save to CD or DVD

2 Click on the Copy to CD link

Copy to CD

3 A balloon appears to notify you that the files have been copied in readiness for being written to CD

> ⓘ **You have files waiting to be written to the CD.** ✕
> To see the files now, click this balloon.

4 Click on the balloon to view the files

5 Click on the "Write these files to CD" link

6 The CD Writing Wizard opens, which takes you through the rest of the CD writing process

Index

191

U

V

W

Z